MI BAD

ROBBERS CUTTHROATS & THIEVES

IN MICHIGAN'S PAST & PRESENT

TOM CARR

AUTHOR OF THE BESTSELLING BLOOD ON THE MITTEN

CHANDLER LAKE BOOKS

Dedicated to Michigan's newspapers, past and present, and their dedicated staffs for guarding democracy, trying to keep leaders honest and recording and preserving history as it happens.

Readers are encouraged to go to www.MissionPointPress.com to find information on how to buy this book in bulk at a discounted rate.

Published by Chandler Lake Books, an Imprint of Mission Point Press

2554 Chandler Lake Rd.
Traverse City, MI 49686

(231) 421-9513

www.MissionPointPress.com

Series editor: Heather Lee Shaw
Book design by Heather Lee Shaw

ISBN: 978-1-943995-83-7

Library of Congress Control Number: 2018956259

Printed in the United States of America.

CHANDLER LAKE

BOOKS

CONTENTS

The first use of a getaway car was in Chantilly, France, in 1911. The Bonnot Gang stole the car the week before robbing Société Générale Bank.

The first successful U.S. bank robbery during peacetime took place in 1866, in Liberty, Missouri. The James-Younger Gang got away with about $60,000 — nearly a million dollars in today's market.

Other robberies occurred earlier, but were said to be committed by Confederate soldiers as an act of war.

Pictured right: Jesse and Frank James.

INTRODUCTION

When I did a talk and signing in Battle Creek for my last book, a woman told me she'd driven an hour from Lansing after a friend of hers read tales from *Blood on the Mitten: Infamous Michigan Murders, 1700s to Present* around a campfire. Her comment crystallized my expectations for these Michigan history/true crime books: I want to make them something people can read out loud, whether by a fire or in the car, all at once or a little at a time. To do that, I've tried to understand the times and places in which these events occurred, then present them in a lively way and in largely modern terms. I've hoped to translate to the reader, in this compilation of dastardly deeds and less than honorable people, Michigan's past and its many textures.

Another remark I've heard from readers is, Why don't I find good people doing good things? Well, while such people and deeds are not the focus here, they are reflected in those who work against the chaos and havoc. Also, I have to qualify the bit about bad people: Yes, these events are bad, and some of the people are downright terrible. However, it also happens that otherwise decent people are driven to crime by mental illness, desperation, or possibly, by a head injury. And those who are bad, are bad in degrees.

In this, my second book for Mission Point Press, the main focus is robbery. It may seem like a step toward less serious crime — less serious in most people's opinion, I hope, than murder. Like a slide from the 5th Commandment down to the 7th; the taking of money rather than the taking of a life. Yet I've found that these stories are just as twisted as the straight murder stories. Which brings me to another difference between this book and the last. Robbery is often a mobile crime, and robbers frequently go long distances for a score or an escape. Michigan may be the point of origin, the point of escape or the scene of a climactic shootout. Either way, there's intrigue all along the way. Besides robbery, I've included other fascinating crimes, like pimping, pirating and jailbreak. And murder. But in these pages, that's the outcome of the crime instead of the main event.

When I speak with readers at bookstores and libraries throughout the state, many ask me which are my favorite stories, or which ones do I find the most compelling. It's always difficult to say. When you spend some time with a story, learning it enough to be able to tell it effectively, they all get under your skin. This time around, though, I have to say the one I feel closest to is that of a man in the late 19th Century who had the same last name as I do. And if you're looking for the worst person to ever grace the Great Lake State, James Carr would definitely be in the running. Carr, with his friend Maggie Duncan, ran a murdering, thieving, kidnapping, bribing and arson-committing enterprise in a lumberjack-era brothel. The shared name is just a coincidence, I swear. Sure, there might be a familial connection way back, since I have some distant roots in upstate New York where he started out. My Carrs, though, came to the Livingston County area of Michigan decades before James Carr left Rochester, New York, for Clare County. Also, lest anyone think he represents dominant traits of all Carrs, I'd like to quote him from court transcripts, a quote that appears later in the book for different reasons: "There's nothing in a name."

In this compilation of stories, some are longer and more detailed than others. The word count and the amount of research varies from story to story. Newspapers have been key in my research, as have books and other written accounts. In some cases, there were slightly differing versions of events, and I've had to decide to which version I would give the most weight. If there's an eyewitness somewhere, I've tended to go with that version, for the immediacy it offers. Then, it necessarily goes through my filter, as I'm the one telling the tales in these pages. If there's a detail that appears differently in another account, I don't always mention that discrepancy or the fact that there is another version out there. In that way, this is not a work of straight journalism, though my back-ground and experience is as a journalist. And even though facts are crucial and my goal always is to be factual, this is not a scholarly work, either, so there are no footnotes. I list sources in the back of the book, though not detail by detail.

I've had to speculate in some parts of the book — not with the larger, more empirical facts, but occasionally with thought processes and with the subtleties of motion. What verbs do I use when I wasn't

Aussie outlaw Ned Kelly (1854 – 1880), attempts to derail a train.

there and when neutral words were often used in the accounts? It's a question I've had to ask myself throughout the process. For instance, would this person in this situation have been more likely to leap, dart, lunge or mosey? I assure you, given the subject matter, this is a book with very little moseying. If an account includes someone shooting a gun out of someone else's hand, I may add a bit of blood to the original, clean description, since it seems to me unlikely that a speeding bullet is going to knock a pistol out of someone's hand without taking a bit of hand with it.

That gets us back to the intent of this book, which is to inform and entertain and, hopefully, put you in the middle of some of the countless compelling experiences within these man-made and natural boundaries that make up the place we call Michigan. And please, don't think I'm calling my state bad, or worse than any other place. I'd move if I thought that. It's just that there's a fascination, and even pride — perverse pride I guess — that makes us want to know of all things good and bad about a place in which we identify. Michigan, to be sure, has not been the home of the best-known crooks. There are no towering figures here, like John Dillinger, Al Capone or Jesse James. Baby Face Nelson is only believed to have pulled off one robbery in this state, but it was a colorful and flawed caper and it made it into these pages. The Wild West is supposed to be where the shootouts and the bawdy houses and the colorful characters abounded in American lore. Yet train and stage-coach robberies also happened under cover of Midwestern woods, not just out on the lonely and rocky expanses of Wyoming or Arizona. The vice and corruption of the ever-moving lumber camps during the white pine boom were every bit as rowdy as the cattle-drives and mining towns of the West.

So, take a look at these pages and get to know just a few of the sinners, and even some saints, that have given the Wolverine State its flavor. And thank you, sincerely, for spending this time with me and my work. Please continue to let me know if I've missed any of the endless episodes that have shaped the lore of this wondrous and sometimes wicked state of ours.

COP AND ROBBER

THE YEAR: 1963
THE CRIME: BANK ROBBERY
THE MOTIVE: LOOKS EASY ENOUGH

SOMETHING ABOUT THAT BANK TOLD ANDY SALKOVICH HE COULD DO IT. He was pretty sure he could walk into the National Bank of Royal Oak, point a gun at a teller, and get out within minutes toting a sack of bills. He should know how it's done. He was a state trooper, after all. And it didn't hurt that he was borrowing another cop's private car — so the plates couldn't be traced back to him.

At age 32, Salkovich had been with the Michigan State Police for seven years and had done little to distinguish himself on the force, supervisors said. He had recently come to the bustling suburban post in Royal Oak, just north of Detroit, and still lived in a bunkhouse with other troopers. Meanwhile, his wife and three young kids were still near the old post in Newaygo, a slopey town 180 miles west-northwest on a wide and steep-shouldered turn of the Muskegon River. Things weren't going so well with the wife and kids. Glenna Salkovich had filed for divorce, charging mental cruelty, just a few days prior. According to some, he hadn't been served divorce papers yet. What's more, they were having a house built in Oak Park, a short commute for Salkovich and a vast improvement over a bunker.

Trooper Salkovich never suggested those problems played into his fateful decision that warm, November Thursday afternoon. But whatever it was, the dangerous whim must have proved irresistible. Shortly after the lunch hour, as he was returning from Oak Park where he had signed papers for the new house, he steadied his nerves enough to walk into the bank and look for the nearest available teller.

Gayle Robinson was behind the teller's window he chose that day. Just 24 and embarking on married life in a tidy and modest Royal Oak neighborhood, she looked out at the lobby as the man with the pug nose, as she later described him, walked up to her window.

"Fill this up," the man demanded, handing her a plastic bag. She glanced down a few inches and a .38-caliber was pointing right at her.

X

She didn't know that this was a state police-issue weapon, intended to protect and serve, not to threaten and rob. In fact, Robinson didn't really know guns and thought it kind of looked like a toy. Still, she knew she'd better do as the man with the gun ordered, and filled the green bag with stacks of green and handed it back through the window.

While that was happening, a customer at the next counter whispered to teller Frank Helsom, "There's a man pointing a gun at the teller next to you."

As the robber turned around to leave, toting $3,156 in the sack — worth over $25,000 in today's economy, nearly half of what he earned in a year — Gayle Robinson, still shaken from looking down the barrel of a gun, turned to her co-worker Helsom and nodded that she'd been robbed.

Helsom was a handsome young man with the standard-issue-1963 haircut, just long enough for the side part to show. At 21, he was four months into married life and a student at Wayne State who had already worked four years at the bank. He sprinted out the door after the robber, in time to see him hop into a black convertible.

Helsom tried to get the license number. He couldn't see it well enough, because the plate had been bent in a way that made it unreadable. As the car sped away, it glanced off another car that was driving into the parking lot. Helsom took a shot at the getaway car and put a ding in the front passenger door. No, not with a gun. Helsom, who had been a multi-sport athlete for the Berkley Bears, threw a rock (some say a brick). He then ran to a nearby drugstore and called the police. As soon as he'd settled down and thought about the fact that he had just chased an armed criminal, he began shaking uncontrollably.

Police quickly circulated a description of the car and the robber to gas stations and body shops in the area, emphasizing the dent in the right door. At Al's Collision, Alex Cutrubes was helping out his son, who owned the business, by minding the shop. An FBI officer came in and asked him to watch out for the black convertible. Shortly after they left, he noticed there was a guy in the waiting room, impatiently pacing back and forth. Cutrubes waited, believing the man was possibly armed, and as soon as the customer left in the freshly-repaired car, Cutrubes called police. Minutes later, two Warren police officers who had just heard the be-on-the-lookout report pulled over a matching car at 13 Mile and Ryan roads. They approached the window and asked for a driver's license. But the driver told them he was one of them, the good guys. With their permission, he reached for his wallet and showed them his state police badge. Well, since he was a cop and there was no dent in the door, they waved him on.

Still, they radioed info about the stop to state police, in accordance with procedure.

THE STATE JOURNAL

HOME EDITION

U. S. Weather Report

Showers tonight, possibly mixed with snow Saturday. Low near 40. High 45.

ONE HUNDRED-NINTH YEAR ★ ★ ★ LANSING—EAST LANSING, MICHIGAN, FRIDAY, NOVEMBER 22, 1963 *44 Pages* UNITED PRESS INTERNATIONAL ASSOCIATED PRESS PRICE—TEN CENTS

KENNEDY IS SLAIN

Trooper Confesses Bank 'Job'

Tossed Rock Assists In Officer's Arrest For $3,156 Holdup

CENTER LINE (AP)—A rock thrown by a bank teller led to the arrest of a state policeman on bank robbery charges Thursday night, and the trooper remorsefully admitted the $3,156 holdup, his superiors said.

Andy J. Salkovich, 32, a seven-year veteran of the force, was arrested at the Center Line state police post.

"If I could tell you why, I'd tell you—I just don't know," he told State Police Capt. Fred Davids.

Frank E. Helsom, bank teller, chased Salkovich from the National Bank of Royal Oak after the robbery Thursday afternoon and threw a rock that dented his car, police said.

A citizen told police which way the car had gone, and officers alerted repair shops in the area. Al Cutrubes Sr. called to report the car had been in his repair shop and gave police the license number, officers said.

"A HARD TIME"

Salkovich, married and father of three children, was arraigned on a bank robbery charge today before U.S. District Judge Fred W. Kaess in Detroit. His

TPR. ANDY J. SALKOVICH

* * *

Bank Job Sad Story For Childs

By DICK FRAZIER
Journal Staff Writer

He looked limp, like a man who had just lost his job.

Commissioner Joseph A. Childs of the Michigan State Police sat at his desk, cupped his chin in his hand, and managed to manufacture the faintest hint of the smile that is so characteristic of him.

JUST BEFORE PRESIDENT WAS KILLED — This is believed to be one of the last pictures taken of President Kennedy before he was slain in his "bubble-top" limousine Friday in Dallas, Texas. He is shown riding in a motorcade about one minute before the bullets were fired at him and Gov. John Connally of Texas. Mrs. Kennedy and Mrs. Connally are also in the car. (AP Wirephoto)

Assassin Also Hits Connally

DALLAS, Texas (AP)—A Secret Service agent and a Dallas policeman were shot and killed today some distance from the area where President Kennedy was assassinated.

No other information was immediately available.

By MERRIMAN SMITH

DALLAS (UPI) — President Kennedy was assassinated today in a burst of gunfire in downtown Dallas. Texas Gov. John Connally was shot down with him.

The President cradled in his wife's arms, had been rushed in his blood-spattered limousine to Parkland Hospital and taken to an emergency room. An urgent call went out for neurosurgeons and blood.

The President, 46 years old, was shot once in the head. Connally was hit in the head and wrist.

Rifle Found

Police found a foreign-make rifle. Sheriff's officers were questioning a young man picked up at the scene.

The President was conscious as he arrived at the hospital. Father Huber from Holy Trinity Roman Catholic Church was called and administered the last rites of the church.

Vice President Lyndon B. Johnson, who now becomes President of the United States, was in a car be-

The gumshoes trying to piece the puzzle together called in the plates to headquarters. It wasn't long before they came to the queasy conclusion that it was one of their own. Patrol cars in the area converged on the Center Line state police post barracks, east of Royal Oak. Salkovich was there, and as he saw them marching toward him, he broke down, sobbing. They gave him some space, but watched him closely. As soon as he could speak, he confessed to the crime and took them to the suitcase in his room, where he'd stashed the banded cash from the National Bank of Royal Oak.

Police were stunned and saddened that one of their own had committed the brazen felony. Mostly, they were embarrassed to have it splashed across headlines. Yet, as it turned out, the attention only lasted a few hours. See, the robbery and arrest took place on November 21, 1963. That meant that it hit the newspapers on November 22. And by about 2 p.m., it was all but forgotten. That's when news of President John F. Kennedy's assassination hit the airwaves. In fact, later news stories about Salkovich's short transit through the United States District Court, guilty plea and five-year prison sentence were relegated to short blurbs, often on inside pages.

Why did he do it? "There has got to be an answer somewhere, but I haven't got one," he said. "I did this on impulse. I was driving from Oak Park where I had gone to sign some papers for the house we were having built there. I must have looked at half a dozen banks. Then I saw this one in Royal Oak and I made up my mind to rob it."

Seems his mind was more madeup than his plans.

BUYING THE FARM

THE YEAR: 1932
THE CRIME: ARMED ROBBERY, MURDER
THE MOTIVE: BIG PAYDAYS, LONG COOLDOWNS

THE CHEVROLET STOPPED ON MAIN STREET AND TWO MEN BOUNDED UP THE STEPS TO THE STONE BUILDING.

Clarkston sits in that stretch among the lakes, woods and hills between Detroit and Flint. In the early 1930s, the factories in those two gritty, world-driving, lunch-bucket towns were running at a fraction of what they had been during the roaring '20s. So the farms and depot towns between them were also hurting.

In Clarkston, downtown stores and the bank were extending Saturday hours, trying to squeeze a little blood from the turnip that was the average pocket or purse in those days. Being a sweaty, slow July evening, stores had their front and back doors open. Fans whirred, menacing to mothers scuttling children around town. These fans were the all-metal jobs, built like tanks and with wide-set grille wires just daring little fingers to take a poke at the spinning blades.

Then a gunshot broke the languid spell. Heads jerked towards the sound. It was the bank. Another gunshot shortly thereafter and Charles Huntley peeked out of his drug store. He saw two guys with guns and a weighty bag sprinting out to the Chevy.

Huntley grabbed his army rifle, and as the punks' car kicked up gravel heading south, the ex-cop fired off two shots. Both hit the car, and one whizzed just inches from the robbers' heads.

Huntley and the rest of the Main Street crowd soon focused their attention on the scene of the crime. They discovered, to their relief, that nobody had been hurt.

THE ROBBERS HAD COME IN, GUNS DRAWN, AND SAID "WE MUST HAVE YOUR CASH!"

Then, Ben Dillon and Leo Bogert herded employees and customers into a back room while Bogert found the bank president and a cashier. He took them to stand with the others, all with their hands up.

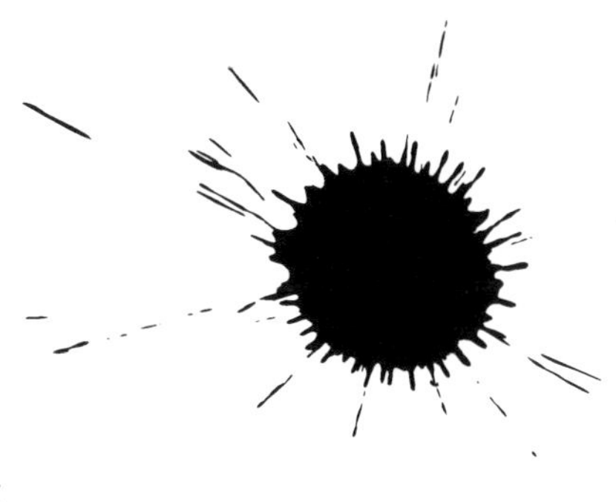

Dillon leaped onto the counter and climbed over the glass to where two tellers were still standing. He began scooping money into a canvas bank sack, jabbering away flirtatiously with one of the tellers, Isabelle King. But he was grabbing money while carelessly waving his gun around, and he accidentally squeezed off a shot. A bullet shattered a ceramic finger-wetter. Undeterred, he asked to be shown into the vault, where he grabbed more loot. And his trigger-finger did it again — the gun went off, pinging the floor.

People outside now scurried behind cars and doorways, and peered at the bank, where they saw through the window hands go up in surrender to the guys with the guns.

DILLON AND BOGERT SPED OUT AND HUNTLEY'S BULLET SHATTERED THEIR REAR WINDOW. As they blasted southward on Main, an off-duty deputy and two other men jumped into a car with their handy rifles and followed their dust through winding roads. Police got word and squealed their tires and kicked up gravel to catch up with the chase.

About four miles out of town, the dust ahead of the vigilantes and cops cleared and police and posse realized that Dillon and Bogert had skipped off to the side somewhere. They turned around and began checking out the forest two-tracks. With precious minutes ticking away, they scanned for clues in the turnoffs. An hour and a half had passed since the robbery. Then, look, over there, a glimpse of a fender. Patrolmen jumped out of their cars and cleared away the brush. Sure enough, it was the Chevy with the shot-out window.

Oakland County Sheriff Frank Schram sped up from Pontiac and took charge. The trail led toward a swamp and if they acted fast, they could surround it and grab the robbers as soon as they got tired of living with lily pads and leeches. Cop cars and armed citizens were still driving there from the towns and sheriff outposts all over the county. Schram stationed cars at curves and intersections, as others inched further toward the mosquito-ruled marsh, hoping to flush out the bandits — with considerable help from the blood-sucking insects, of course.

A COUPLE HUNDRED OR SO COPS CAME FROM PONTIAC, DETROIT, FLINT, EVEN YPSILANTI AND LANSING. All the top brass quickly conferred and assigned the troops to their posts. They lit it up with headlights and searchlights, waiting for hungry, depleted and defeated crooks to stagger out of their slimy hell.

They staked out and sweated in their uniforms. They milled about, traded war stories and sent go-fers to town for thermoses of coffee. They waited and glanced at their watches so they'd know what time to type on the report as to when they cuffed the criminals. Midnight came, then the wee hours. A lot of sighs and a lot of pacing. As an orange sun began to lift the mist off the swamp, the waiting party began to thin out. It was becoming clear that the crooks had never even run into the wetland. Still, an ever-shrinking crew stayed on for another day, before a few armed civilians picked up the vigil.

In fact, while the police were still setting up at their waiting posts, the bandits were divvying up the loot somewhere in the next county to the north, Lapeer. The traffic of eager officers likely stomped and drove over any tracks that might've told the real story. See, the two young criminals stole the Chevy earlier that afternoon in Pontiac. That's the car everybody saw them speed off in. But after they parked it, they did not make a panicked escape on foot into muck and cattails. They had actually stashed another vehicle there, which nobody was looking for. After hiding the Chevy, they tossed the bag of cash into the waiting car, then peeked out as the parade of pursuers sped around the bend. They turned the car toward town and made a leisurely and nonchalant getaway, minding the speed limit, like all law-abiding citizens. They may have even passed late-coming police cars without being noticed.

ABOUT A MONTH LATER, THE EXECUTOR OF THE WILLIAM STRATTON ESTATE MUST HAVE SAT UP IN HIS CHAIR, WHEN SPRY, SLIGHT CLAUDIA DILLON PULLED OUT A ROLL OF BILLS, ENOUGH TO BUY THE LATE STRATTON'S FARMHOUSE, BARN, SHEDS AND ACREAGE. Any interested customer with cash was welcome at a time when foreclosing on property was one of the few growth industries. So seeing the woman count out $2,000 into his palm brightened his day. Still, he had to wonder, how did she get that kind of money? Her son, she explained, flew stunt planes. He was a flight instructor, killed a year earlier in a plane crash. This wad of bills was the insurance money, she claimed. If the man selling the farm had wanted to look it up, through the newspapers at the library or at the paper's office, he would have found that Jay Dillon had indeed died a year earlier after his small plane spiraled to the ground while taking an aviation student for a short flight at the Pontiac municipal airport. The gentleman representing the old Stratton place counted out the "insurance" money and signed the deed over to the Dillons.

Claudia moved into the home with her two surviving sons, Ben and Scott. With Ben came his girlfriend, Marion Halliday, who was 17 and recuperating from minor injuries when Ben took his motorcycle into a skid with her riding on back. Ben stuffed a good chunk of his robbery money, from Clarkston and other jobs, into a jar and buried it in the barn. The family figured they could stay on the farm, lay low and not attract too much attention.

Claudia, a wiry and athletic woman, was perfectly at home with the pastoral life. She knew animals, because she'd been a stunt rider for a circus. Ben and Scott also settled into farm life. If any of them might have stood out in the rural setting, it was Marion Halliday. She had lived in Toronto and had seen a bit of the world. Young and stylish, some media would later refer to her as Ben's gun moll.

They weren't living the most flamboyant lives imaginable, by any means. Yet this was the Great D, when Ben's purchase of the best radio sold on Main Street must have looked like quite the extravagance. He bought a new car, one of the nicer ones on the Hudson dealer's lot. And his girlfriend was dressed to the nines while others were just trying to stay clothed.

The farm, about 10 miles north of Lapeer, was home to them for the next three months. Sure, they were enjoying the rural life, but Ben Dillon, who had once said he never wanted to be poor again, was thinking of pulling another job. The Clarkston heist had been at least his second successful, high-yield robbery. He'd also held up the General Motors Truck Company and gotten out with $2,800.

He told his brother that he planned to make the farmhouse his hideout. He'd wander away from there, pull bank jobs far away, then hopefully outrun the heat to come back to an ordinary, out-of-the-way farm. The perfect combination: Excitement there and a place to catch a million breaths here. Soon, he planned to head straight for the dust bowl and pull off a job in Tulsa, Oklahoma.

WHILE THE DILLONS HOPED THE LOCAL MEMORY OF THE CLARKSTON ROBBERY WOULD COOL DOWN, IT REMAINED RED HOT FOR FRANK GREENAN. The fiasco of the swamp stake-out stung and embarrassed him as second-in-command of the Oakland County Sheriff's Department. He'd lived with his mother since his wife died, and he had one goal to reach in his career. After climbing up the ranks to undersheriff, he was now looking to shed the "under" part of his title. Sheriff Frank Schram was retiring and Greenan was running to replace him in the election that fall on the Republican ticket. He should be a shoo-in. Yet he feared that when the good citizens drove past his campaign signs, they'd think about him and his boss commanding armies to surround an enemy who was already long gone. What's more, Franklin Roosevelt was the one who seemed to be getting people excited at the top of the ballot, and he might drag some voters over to the Democrats' side, even for sheriff. So Greenan had eagerly followed leads in the robbery for three months, but they'd all come up dry. It had gotten to be just a week before election day, and he would love to bring in the cuffed robbers in front of news cameras, flashing their bulbs away and leaving spots before everyone's eyes.

It was the first of November when a 15-year-old boy came in with a tip. Seems the lad had worked for the Dillons when they'd lived in Pontiac. Tongues back there were now wagging that the Dillons had left out of the blue, and rumor had it that they paid cash for their new homestead. Plus, Ben had a spoiled girlfriend and he took her out on the town looking a little too just right.

Greenan had received some other tips leading up to this, so he was hopeful, but realistic. Still, the kid seemed honest and earnest, and said he'd been spooked into coming forward when Ben had schemed about taking the kid on a heist. So Greenan called in Deputy Harvey Tedder, the father of ten children with an eleventh mouth to feed coming within days. Tedder was a trustworthy cop and one Greenan hoped to take with him as he moved up the ladder. He also called the bank up in Clarkston and arranged to pick up the president and a clerk to confirm that Dillons were, indeed, the robbers. And, he called Sheriff Byron Courter of Lapeer County, because, well, the bad guys were now in his backyard.

AFTER A FRAUGHT AND BUMPY RIDE UP TO THE FARM, THE TWO SHERIFF'S CARS TURNED IN TO THE DRIVEWAY. They faced two guys sweating as they chopped away at wood, stocking up for the winter. As the brakes squeaked to a stop, the woodchoppers looked up at them and at the six-pointed stars painted on the car doors. Those doors were barely open when the bank cashier blurted out, "That's them!" Ben dropped his axe and sprinted toward the house, while Scott made for a tool shed.

Greenan and Tedder were quick on the draw and fired shots that just missed Ben as he leaped onto the porch and bolted inside the house. They ran up to the doorway and were just inside when Ben grabbed a shotgun, wheeled around and fired. The seasoned cops shot back, and as lead flew in every direction, Greenan took a shoulder-full of shot that blew him backwards, stumbling out the door. As he fell into the yard, another slug ripped the gun out of his hand in a spray of blood. Hubbell and Courter hoisted Greenan into a squad car and told the bankers to get him to a hospital — and themselves out of here.

Across the yard, Deputy Clare Hubbell sneaked over to the tool shed door. Led by his pistol, he turned into the doorway where Scott, unarmed, put up his hands and then gave up his wrists for the heavy-metal bracelets. Hubbell slapped one of them on, then yanked him over to a cop car and clanked the other ring around the bumper.

Lapeer Sheriff Courter was trying to keep cover while edging toward the house where a barrage of gun blasts had just filled the air. He jerked

SURVIVOR of a death battle in a farmyard seven miles from Lapeer Wednesday morning, Scott Dillon was taken to the Oakland County Jail by Detective Nelson Singleton. Dillon's brother Ben committed suicide after murdering Oakland County Undersheriff Frank Greenan and Deputy Harvey Tedder when they tried to arrest the brothers.

Detroit Free Press; Nov 3,1932.

as he saw a pair of eyes, wide and startled, peeking out the door. It was Claudia. She vaulted over the porch and dashed across the grass, holding her dress up a bit to clear her long strides. Courter had the angles on his side — he jumped in front of her and tackled her, both of them sliding along the grass.

After Deputy Hubbell cuffed Scott Dillon to the car, he spotted young Marion the "Moll" hiding in the yard. He grabbed her and held her in front of himself to catch any gunfire that might come their way. He pushed her toward the house and shoved her into the now-too-quiet doorway. Marion frantically called out, "Don't shoot, Ben! It's me, Marion."

Hubbell pushed on, and that's when they saw Tedder, face down in a pool of blood, moaning. Then a shot went off. In another room, Ben Dillon lay with a half-bloody face. He was rushed to a hospital in Lapeer, but died within an hour. It was widely assumed to be a suicide, though some believed it was an accident — after all, he was the guy who fumbled off two nervous shots while robbing the bank.

Undersheriff Greenan, Deputy Tedder and Dillon all died that day, leaving very different legacies. Greenan and Tedder were honored with huge funerals attended by police from throughout the state. Greenan's replacement on the ballot for sheriff was elected. Tedder's wife gave birth to a baby girl, and received an $18 weekly pension from Oakland County to raise the 11 kids without their father. That's about $330 today.

Police took turns interrogating Claudia and Scott Dillon and Marion Halliday. They soon determined that Scott was telling the truth in that he was not the second holdup man. They even put Marion in a lineup for witnesses, wondering if the accomplice could have been her, dressed as a man. When they questioned Claudia, she actually confessed that she knew all along about her son being a bank robber.

Meanwhile, department sleuths searched through photos that they'd found back at the blood-soaked farmstead for evidence. They came across a snapshot — black-and-white, of course — with Ben and Marion standing in front of a car. Luckily, police could make out the license plate numbers. They called up state offices and had them search through the file cabinets for that number. Turns out, it was registered to a man by the name of Leo Bogert. They showed Mrs. Dillon the photo and told her the name. Did it ring a bell? Yeah, that's the guy he talked about, she said. That's the one who robbed the bank with him.

Police detectives tracked Bogert to his brother Ellwood's home in Vassar, east of Saginaw. They drove up just as he was about to skip town. He had truly lain low the last three months, unlike his accomplice. He'd buried $2,000 in a jar under a rain spout at another brother's farm a couple miles east of Kingston. He'd read of Ben's death in the paper and figured he'd be feeling some heat soon. Now, police cars were clogging the driveway he needed to back out of. He put his hands in the air and, as Deputy Hubbell patted down his pockets, two handkerchiefs full of bills were discovered, musty and stained from being in the leaky jar.

The Lapeer County Press and Clarion has him saying, "Aw, what's the use. I did it," a rather modest response for a guy who'd committed armed robbery. Well, armed, but not loaded, he told the interrogators. He said only Ben's revolver was loaded. He also told them Ben had bragged about a GM Truck & Coach Corp. office payroll robbery he'd pulled off in broad daylight two years earlier for nearly three grand. Finally, he claimed that the Clarkston crime had been gnawing at him and he'd wanted to come in and confess. "I was afraid to, because I knew if I did, Ben would kill me."

Leo Bogert was sentenced to 30 years in prison, but that was later reduced to 10.

THE ROBBIN' HOOD FOLK HERO >>>>>>>>>>

Daddy was a bankrobber
But he never hurt nobody
He just loved to live that way
And he loved to steal your money

—THE CLASH "Bankrobber"

Many a starving farmer
The same old story told
How the outlaw paid their mortgage
And saved their little homes

Others tell you 'bout a stranger
That come to beg a meal,
Underneath his napkin
Left a thousand dollar bill

—WOODY GUTHRIE "Pretty Boy Floyd"

JOHN DILLINGER — THE ELVIS OF 1930s BANK ROBBERS — WAS SOMETIMES CHEERED BY AUDIENCES WHEN HIS EXPLOITS MADE THE MOVIE-THEATER NEWSREELS. The Hoosier outlaw was a bit of a bad-boy reality star to ordinary folk facing foreclosure. They had little reason to sympathize with the banks sending them threatening letters.

That's not to say that people actually wanted their sons or daughters to go into this line of work. Daring stick-up artists were always one dead cop or bystander away from unforgiven villainy. Take handsome young Ben Dillon, who is said to have leaped over the bank counter window before Dillinger made it seem cool, blew his chance at being a darkly romantic figure when he committed a double-murder/suicide.

Dillinger is said to have never hit a Michigan bank for fear — or respect — of the sometimes-paid vigilante mobs that often hopped right into action when the alarm sounded (see "Paid Posses"). Or maybe he knew what a PR disaster it would be to have to pick off civilians. But people loved reading stories about Indiana's favorite wayward son — like how he escaped from jail and supposedly serenaded a getaway hostage with popular songs before dropping him off 50 miles from the clink. The police helped build his legend when they mentioned that the escape

The FBI killing of John Dillinger on July 22, 1934, attracted quite the crowd.

weapon was a gun carved out of soap or wood and colored with shoe polish. That was a lie, some now say. The police may have made it up so they didn't have to admit that one of their turnkeys had accepted a bribe.

Dillinger was just one of several legendary bankrobbers to hit the Midwest in the Depression. Bonnie and Clyde took glamorous photos of each other with their cars and guns. Thirty years after their bullet-riddled deaths, they seemed dangerously cool again when Faye Dunaway and Warren Beatty played them on the big screen. Certain outlaws' nicknames — like Baby Face and Pretty Boy — added an appealing yin-yang contrast to how they made their inevitably short, but exciting livings. Speaking of Pretty Boy Floyd, the Oklahoman is said to have paid off mortgages for some destitute, dust-bowl farmers, cementing the loyalty of citizens who might be asked by the cops, *Which way did he go?* Dillinger bought the admiration of common folk for a much lower price: he supposedly liked to treat the kiddies to a round of ice cream every now and then.

Of course, the image and myth of the charitable robber is always a re-telling of Robin Hood, the 500-year-old English folk hero gone global. But these guys weren't like the hero of Sherwood Forest. They were keeping most of the loot and living the high-octane life of a gambling, whoring, sometimes killing, gangster. For that, they generally enjoyed the utmost respect within the criminal underworld. They were the high rollers, who strutted their stuff in front of crooks engaged in less dramatic pursuits.

Decades before the Great Depression, Jesse James achieved something akin to that stardom in the 1870s and 80s. He's sometimes romanticized, though several people died as a result of James-Younger Gang crimes. He and brother Frank robbed banks, stagecoaches, trains and carnivals. They also killed an engineer by derailing his train. And when they found the express car carried a fraction of what they'd hoped, they collected cash, jewelry and watches from the passengers.

Like many of the ilk, James met a bloody end. And his betrayer, Robert Ford, became more infamous than the outlaw he shot in the back of the head when he accepted a reward from the governor.

Of course not all fascination is admiration, but the interest has certainly followed them after their deaths. When Dillinger was gunned down in Chicago with his Woman in Red, curiosity seekers gathered for a free look at the corpse, both before and after the undertakers made it less gruesome. What's more, Dillinger's father went on the road with some of his late son's personal artifacts to entertain curious audiences around the Midwest. Reality TV without the TV.

On Dillinger's last night of life, he attended the 8:30 show at the Biograph Theater with his girlfriend Polly Hamilton and Ana Sage, aka Ana Ivanova Akalieva. Sage was a Romanian immigrant threatened with deportation for "low moral character." She offered agents information on Dillinger for a promise to stop her deportation. (Sage and Hamilton were roommates.) The FBI agreed to her terms, but later reneged and deported her anyway.

Sage is popularly known as The Woman in Red. In fact, her dress was orange — but The Woman in Orange doesn't quite spin in the right direction, does it?

HELPING DILLINGER

THE YEAR: 1934
THE CRIME: JAILBREAK, MURDER
THE MOTIVE: NOTHING TO LOSE

JOHN DILLINGER'S LEGENDARY JAIL ESCAPE IN NORTHERN INDIANA (SEE PAGE 11), WOULD NOT HAVE BEEN POSSIBLE WITHOUT THE HELP OF AN UNSUNG CRIMINAL WHO FLED TO PORT HURON AND TOOK MAYHEM WITH HIM.

Herbert Youngblood was born in Louisiana and had already served time in prison when he came to the acrid, steel mill city of Gary, Indiana, in the early 1930s. In 1933, he walked into Piazza Produce, where the owner, Tony Piazza was hosting a poker game in the back of the store. Youngblood pulled a gun and ordered them to hand over the whole pot. Tony refused to ante up, so Youngblood shot him to death. At the age of 29 or 35, depending on the source, Youngblood was facing charges of first-degree murder and armed robbery.

And that's how he happened to occupy the Second Empire-style brick edifice known as Crown Point Jail, a few cells down from John Dillinger.

After Dillinger persuaded a turnkey to let him out of the cell, he asked if any other inmates wanted to join him. Youngblood, with little to lose, gladly rose to the opportunity and helped crowd guards into one of the cells they'd just emptied. First, he intimidated hostages — and anyone else standing in the way — with a toilet plunger handle, and then he menaced the staff with one of two Tommy guns Dillinger had grabbed from the warden's office. The two made their way into the garage where there were several getaway cars to choose from. A helpful mechanic provided input, and Dillinger opted for Sheriff Lillian Holley's Ford with a powerful V-8 engine.

Taking a deputy and the sheriff's mechanic as hostages — plus an armed Youngblood to keep them from trying anything funny — Dillinger drove through town and out to country roads so he could criss-cross his way into Illinois.

X

They drove 50 miles or so from the jail — stopping once to dismount the flashing light that identified it as a police car and to put on tire chains to gain traction in the roads muddied up from relentless March rains. Then, Dillinger dropped the hostages off and gave them $4 to find their way back.

As they angled toward some of the Public Enemy's friends in the Windy City, Dillinger told Youngblood to crouch low between the front and back seats so he wouldn't attract attention. Finally, at a streetcar stop on Western Avenue in Chicago, Dillinger gave Youngblood $100 and the two parted ways. In addition to the monetary reward, Dillinger later repaid Youngblood's invaluable help in the escape by explaining his willingness with this insult: "You know how a n****r is."

While Dillinger reconvened with thug friends for more bank robberies, Youngblood hopped trains into Michigan and headed for Detroit and then Port Huron, Michigan's Thumb-knuckle. He figured that if the heat got turned up, the Canadian border town would allow him an easy escape across the St. Clair River. (Port Huron's narrow-river border, like Detroit's, had allowed for easy liquor-smuggling during Prohibition.)

Youngblood went to the part of the city where he'd apparently hoped to blend in — to the south side, an industrial area with a growing black population. Still, his personality was the opposite of incognito. His thirst for booze and his hunger for notoriety created a heat of its own. He's said to have spent a good deal of his short stay in Port Huron drinking and bragging about his brief association with the infamous JD. Police even received a call from someone in the neighborhood known as South Park, saying there was a "suspicious colored man" flashing a revolver and a wad of cash and bragging that he'd escaped from jail somewhere.

What finally did him in, was when he staggered into an African American-owned grocery store at 2925 Moak Street, drunk and knocking merchandise off shelves. He grabbed a pack of cigarettes and refused to pay, prompting Eugene Fields, the teenage son of store-owner, Pearl Abraham, to call the police. When the sheriff and two underlings arrived, he submitted to a pat-down. They frisked him and found a .38 caliber automatic. They also (wrongly) assumed that was the only gun he carried. As they prepared to arrest Youngblood, he pulled a .32 Savage automatic out of his pocket and opened fire. Roy Parks, working behind the counter, hit the floor and felt his heart thump while rapid gunfire burst out on the other side. Eugene Fields kept his feet nearby, unarmed. "The bandit got in two shots to their one, when the shooting started," he told reporters later. "The officers were damn slow."

Youngblood's shots hit both of Undersheriff Charles Cavanaugh's lungs, as well as one lung of Deputy Edward Lohr. Youngblood took some lead from the cops, too, but stayed standing while he managed to land shots on all three officers at least once. A wounded cop dropped a gun and Fields dove between the legs of a standing officer to grab it. He shot Youngblood twice. When Youngblood returned fire, he hit the young man's right shoulder and both Fields and Youngblood went down.

Dillinger Negro Aide Dies after Gun Fight with Michigan Police

HERBERT YOUNGBLOOD

JOHN DILLINGER

Youngblood of Gary, Ind., who accompanied Dillinger on flight from the Crown Point, Ind., jail, was fatally wounded by police guns at Port Huron, Friday, after an attempt to escape capture there. Youngblood's confession before he died that Dillinger and two other men were in the vicinity of Port Huron sent all available state police and sheriff's officers in search for the desperado, (Story on Page 1).

Lansing State Journal; Mar 16, 193

FORMER SHERIFF WILLIAM L. VanANTWERP looks at clippings from The Times Herald in his scrapbook telling of the shooting of Dillinger henchman Herbert Youngblood, March 16, 1934. The shooting occurred in the building behind Mr. VanAntwerp at Moak and Thirtieth Streets. At that time it housed a candy and tobacco store. Now it is an apartment dwelling. (Times Herald Staff Photo by Ralph W. Polovich).

The Times Herald; Jul 12, 1964.

Cavanaugh died the next day, while the other lawmen and Fields survived their wounds.

Youngblood was taken to Port Huron Hospital with six to ten new holes in his body. Slipping away from life, he asked for a Catholic priest to pray with him and give him last rites. The priest granted him conditional absolution, or the forgiveness of his sins, on the condition that he cooperate with police. While officers searched Port Huron's underground haunts for Public Enemy #1, the priest repeatedly told the mortally wounded criminal that he could cross over to the next life with a clean slate if *only* he would help police catch the bad man. Youngblood pleaded, uttering over and over, "Pray for me Father," as the priest leaned in to catch his dying words. Youngblood did end up whispering that Dillinger had crossed the river and was heading further into Canada. That information was probably not absolution-worthy, since it was false. Yet it was all Youngblood was giving, not wanting to die a rat, even to a disloyal criminal superstar.

In reality, Dillinger had gone northwest, not northeast. He would rob banks in South Dakota and Iowa and survive a shootout with the FBI in Minnesota before the month was over. Even so, he had only about four months left before his end outside the Biograph Theater in Chicago, accompanied by the "Woman in Red," an FBI informant.

IMMACULATELY CONCEIVED

THE YEAR: 2000
THE CRIME: CLANDESTINE CHRISTMAS CAPER
THE MOTIVE: NOT FRANKINCENSE OR MYRRH

WHEN POLICE DROVE BY A COMERICA BANK AT WOODWARD AND SQUARE LAKE ROAD AFTER MIDNIGHT ON CHRISTMAS MORNING, IT APPEARED THAT NOT A CREATURE WAS STIRRING. An alarm had gone off about 1 a.m., so the police had swung by the bank and made a loop around the drive-through lane. No signs of life in the non-descript branch bank in this toney, north-side suburb. An hour later, a bank security officer took a look and came to the same conclusion — all was well.

Even the next day, nothing appeared to be out of order, although the bank was closed for the holidays. And then, on Tuesday, December 26, an ATM technician on a routine service call arrived before opening time. He stuck his key in the lock and it wouldn't fit. Bending down to take a closer look, he saw there was a piece of copper wire jammed right where the key was supposed to go. After he worked the wire out of the lock, he let himself into the building and discovered tools lying around. He saw scratches and grind marks on an automatic teller machine and a vault. Seemed burglars had worked on them both with heavy-duty power tools, but they hadn't, apparently, had any luck. The vault and the cash vendor remained stubbornly intact and closed.

Of course, the technician immediately called police, and that's when things got really interesting. First, officers discovered that they had incorrectly labeled that alarm "false" on the 24th. When they drove through that night, they didn't see any sign of a jimmied door because the burglars had, in fact, broken a big window to get inside. And, in a clever and artistic bit of preparation, they had replaced the broken window with an exact-sized piece of plywood, decorated to look like the break-room curtains complete with Christmas decorations, including a large elf holding a sack of toys. They apparently worked fast to get the fake window in place and likely took a break when police drove up in response to the alarm.

X

The crooks toiled away for some time in their futile struggles against the safe and the ATM, but when they failed to score there, they looked elsewhere. Bonanza! After prying open the drawer that dispensed the cash to the teller windows, they helped themselves to $123,000 in bills, equal to about $180,000 today. On their way out, they carefully disconnected another alarm and left it in a sink.

The Bloomfield Township police and the FBI were impressed, but there was something just too perfect about the job. The knowledge of which window to break (it was the employee break room, on the same side of the bank as the drive-through window) and the alarm system pointed to an inside job. Officials interviewed and re-interviewed all the bank employees. None of them sounded suspicious. Detectives combed reports from other jurisdictions for any similar bank robberies. Nothing really fit the methods of this break-in. All the questioning and sleuthing came up dry. There were no fingerprints on the discarded tools left behind, no footprints in the snow and the imprint of where they had apparently set down the 3-foot by 5-foot window-replacement also led nowhere.

Days, weeks, months went by and no good leads, not even with a $10,000 reward dangling out there. Detectives kept their eyes on the bank employees, but no new, flashy cars arrived in the parking lot, nor were there any other signs that an employee had gotten a large windfall of cash.

Years went by and the case went cold. Other than perhaps a begrudging respect for the criminals, the cops and the bank had nothing. That left them to wonder not only how, but why. Why would someone pull off a meticulously prepared one-off crime like this? Perhaps it was gambling debt, or maybe someone who owed money to dangerous people. Maybe it was the thrill of it or a personal dare. They might have bought some really nice Christmas gifts that year, whoever it was. And maybe they simply did it because they figured they could.

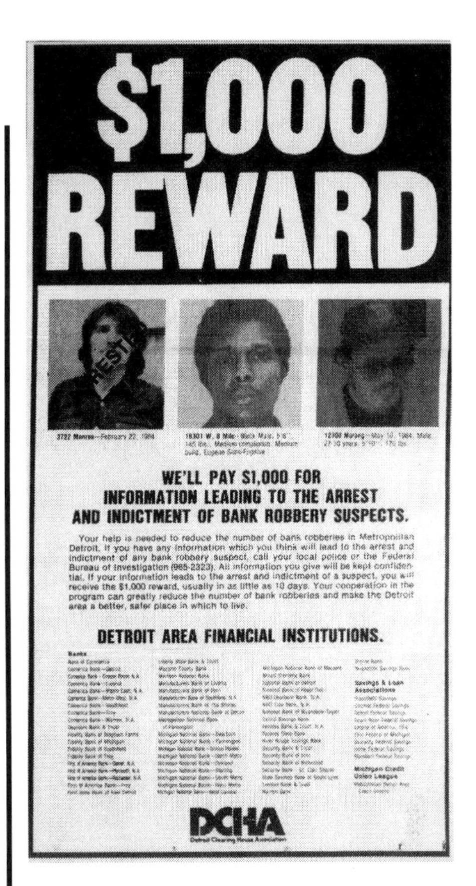

So you want to rob a bank? You may want to find out how much more likely you are to end up in prison than in a luxury hideout sipping 20-year-old Scotch after the heist.

According to the FBI, about twice as likely. Bank robberies have about a 60 percent chance of being solved, higher than most other crimes. The rate for robbers themselves getting caught are actually much higher, and according to some figures, is well over 90 percent. That's because there are only a few successful criminals in the field who pull off a number of heists. Most are not so lucky, or so slick.

Police and robbers say the reasons for getting caught include not being well prepared enough and having too many people involved. When there's more than one crook, there's more than one to screw it up — and blab about it.

VIGILANTE M.D.

THE YEAR: 1930
THE CRIME: BANK HOLDUP BY GANG
THE MOTIVE: 4 GUYS, 4 MOTIVES, ALL BAD

WORD GOT AROUND FAST IN MANCELONA ON THAT JUNE DAY OF 1930. SIRENS WENT OFF IN TOWN. SCHOOL KIDS RAN TO THE WINDOWS. CLERKS, POTATO FARMERS AND EVEN DOCTORS RAN OUT OF THEIR STORES, FIELDS AND OFFICES TO CHASE SOMETHING A BIT MORE EXCITING THAN THEIR DAILY TOILS.

It was between 9 and 10 in the morning, and four men had just held up Antrim County State Savings Bank. They'd hopped out of their car with bandanas covering their noses and mouths, and while one of them stayed outside to keep anyone else from coming in, the other three ran in and lined up the bank tellers against a wall. Just to show they were dead serious, they forced a couple and their daughter to lie face down on the floor throughout the terrifying ordeal.

With a take of $1,000 or so (about $14,000 now), they piled back into their 1928 Chevrolet sedan — a car said to be able to hit speeds of 65 mph and more — and zipped westward through town, but not before Herb Sullivan had stepped out into the street, firing at the car with a rifle. Sullivan was a clerk nearby at Medalie's Store, which sold clothing and fabrics and still sometimes referred to them as dry goods. He had experience with firearms, having fought in the World War, and on this occasion became the first of hundreds of citizens to take up arms that morning. In this case — and the figures may be somewhat inflated for the sake of good folklore — it's said that 1,000 vigilantes from Mancie and surrounding towns grabbed their guns to go after the culprits.

As the getaway car turned north onto Cedar River Road, Dr. L.G. Rifenberg was persuaded to go after them in his Ford Coupe. Sullivan and another armed man hopped onto the car's running board and off they went.

LANSING, MICHIGAN, TUESDAY, JUNE 3, 1930

State Troopers from East Lansing Post Flew To Antrim County Monday to Hunt Bandits

Here are officers of the Michigan state police just before they took off in an airplane from the Capital City airport here Monday afternoon for Bellaire on a hunt for the bandits who Monday morning robbed the Antrim County Savings bank at Mancelona.

Shown in the picture above are Commissioner Oscar G. Olander, at the extreme left, Capt. John Cleghorn, commander of the uniform division of the state police, and Troopers Prechowiak, Sechrist and Ruhl. Commissioner Olander did not make the trip.

Lansing State Journal, Jun. 3, 1930.

Meanwhile, the crooks pulled into the woods at a low spot on a curve and waited. Another getaway driver was supposed to pick them up. But when Rifenberg's car swung around the bend, they opened fire, hitting Sullivan and knocking him off the running board. He was down but not out, and rolled himself off the road to hide in the brush. Rifenberg raced on to a neighboring home, to ask for help, but when he returned someone had already come by and taken Sullivan into town to have the buckshot removed.

The robbers moved through the woods to keep cover, waiting for an accomplice to come and drive them to safety. The car never arrived. Concealed behind the brush, they watched the flow of pursuers whizzing northward. No one noticed that the robbers hadn't gotten far, and were, indeed, cutting trails rather than taking the main roads.

The posse rushed on another 12 miles or so, converging on the crossroad where Derenzy and Eddy School roads meet, just outside of Bellaire. Word of the robbery had sped around the county and vigilantes from all parts were gearing up for the chase. One of the Bellaire possemen was another physician, Dr. J. Gervers. He and his son Fred had stationed themselves on the intersection, near a farmhouse, ready to head the robbers off should they think of fleeing through their fair town. That's when the real trouble began,

Rifenberg and the others from Mancelona stared across at the Bellaire posse. Both parties believing they were looking at criminals. Before they could make any introductions, a shot went off. Time for talk was over and lead started flying in all directions.

Dr. Gervers was hit in the neck and spine and dropped to the ground. His son bolted past his father to the farmhouse for help and cover. The Mancelona possemen trained their rifles on the house, figuring it was the cowardly robbers who had pulled young Gervers inside. They couldn't see into the home, and as Gervers hid in the basement, the self-deputized armed force outside chipped away at the farmhouse walls with their rifles. Their bullets whizzed over the good doctor, lying wounded in the farmyard. Nobody dared carry him to safety, lest the mysterious thugs waiting in the house open fire on them, or they get hit by over-eager, "friendly" fire.

That went on for two hours, until Sheriff Bill Kittle began to doubt the effectiveness of the current strategy. He knew it was the Lindmer farm, so where was farmer Lindmer? Taking cover as best he could, the sheriff worked his way closer and closer and caught a glimpse through the basement window. Someone was with Gervers' kid, all right. It was farmer Lindmer. The only danger they faced was the trigger-happy mob outside. The sheriff called off the shooting, and the bullets flying toward the home came fewer and fewer as word got out. The fight could have gotten a lot bigger, however, as a plane of state troopers armed with machine guns was en route. They were called off before they arrived. Dr. Gervers was carried to a car and taken to a fellow physician.

THE AFTERNOON AND EVENING WORE ON, WITH LITTLE PROGRESS, BUT AS DARK SETTLED, COPS GOT THEIR FIRST BREAK. Around 10 p.m. or so, a robber named Sylvester Elliott found his way out of his deep-woods hiding spot and stepped out onto Cedar River Road. As soon as he did, he caught a blinding flashlight beam in his eyes. Two policemen, staking out that stretch of road, cuffed him and shoved him in the car. After a quick look around — they didn't see anyone there with him — they drove him back to the bank. Turned out Sylvester had lived in the area before but was now visiting from Kalamazoo to make some quick — but not so easy anymore — money. The two officers led the 22-year-old into the bank and backed him into an office chair. They grilled him, always staying between him and the door, until the sun began lighting up the stores across the street.

Meanwhile, his two brothers and accomplices, Fred and Leonard Elliott, had abandoned their car and, with their stomachs growling after hiking through the woods all night, they put out their dusty thumbs on the road to Alba. They got a ride, hopped out and went into a store, looking at sausages and cheese and fruit and bottles of pop and other portable foods for the fugitive on the go. They were famished and funky and the other customers gave them the side-eye. As soon as they left and the door sprang shut, the whispering hit the ears of a small, eager posse, ready to grab their guns.

The handful of volunteer enforcers trailed the suspicious characters out to the graveyard. There, in some tall grass, they cornered the brothers. The Elliotts stood and fired. The possemen jerked their rifles in place and answered their fire. Vigilantes Robert Kitchen and R.C. Bennett took bullets in painful but not deadly places. Leonard Elliott of the robbing brothers took the worst of it and lost an eye.

The graveyard gunfight ended with their arrest, but there was one other culprit still on the loose. Loren Morrison, who had been going by the name Fred Kelly, a former Kalamazoo police officer, was still hiding out somewhere — probably close by. Seems the Elliott brothers had ditched him, suspicious that he wanted to kill them and take all the loot. Kelly hid out in the woods for a couple of days before catching a train from Alba to Cadillac. Not long after he stepped off the passenger car, police nabbed him.

The criminals were caught, but the money made a break for it. Fred Kelly hid $400, equal to about $6,000 now, in his father's boarding house in Cadillac. That is, he hid it until a pretty, young boarder flirted the young criminal into showing it to her. Then, she and her newlywed husband grabbed it when he wasn't looking and hopped aboard a train to Saginaw. They bought a car and lived it up. By the time police arrested them for accepting stolen property, they'd spent all but $10 of it. Violet Manier, the 18-year-old bride, told cops that Kelly "might as well have" thrown the cash out a train window.

The judge gave each of the four robbers the worst he could: life in prison. Dr. Gervers continued to practice medicine for several more years, though he now did so from a wheelchair.

VIGILANTISM IN THE USA >>>>>>>>

Vigilantism — acting in a law enforcement capacity or in pursuit of perceived justice without legal authority — has been around at least since Biblical times.

The death of Joseph Smith, religious leader and founder of Mormonism and the Latter Day Saints movement, is among the earliest and most infamous incidents of homegrown vigilantism. Smith died on June 27, 1844, when a mob of about 200 armed men, their faces painted black with wet gunpowder, stormed the jail where he was being held on charges of treason against the state of Illinois.

Contemporary vigilante groups in the USA:

- Ranch Rescue: Dedicated to forcibly removing illegal immigrants from private property. Operates in Arizona, California, Colorado, Kentucky, New Mexico, Missouri, Oklahoma, Texas and Virginia. Still in business.
- The Minutemen Project: dedicated to expelling illegal immigrants who cross the Mexico-US border. Still in business.
- Phoenix Jones and the Rain City Superhero Movement: A nonviolent group dedicated to crime prevention. Ceased operations in 2014.

Above: The Bald Knobbers, active in the Ozarks from 1883–1889, were dedicated to aiding law enforcement officials in the protection of life and property and apprehension of criminals.

Below: Phoenix Jones (left, without his superhero mask) in 2013.

TARRING AND FEATHERING OF JOSEPH SMITH.

Joseph Smith was 24 when he published the Book of Mormon. Five years later, he was tarred and feathered and left for dead by a mob of Ohioan vigilantes, furious about his political power and support of communalism.

Smith died, attacked again by vigilantes twelve years later, giving rise to Beaver Island's King Strang (see page 47).

In October 1862, between 150 and 200 suspected Unionists were arrested by Confederate troops around Cooke County, Texas. Some were tried by a "Citizen's Court" organized by a Confederate officer, although this "court" had no legal status in Texas. Forty-one of the suspected Unionists were executed in Gainesville, one or two at a time, by hanging. The Great Hanging at Gainesville is claimed to be the largest mass hanging in the history of the United States.

PAID POSSES >>>>>>>>>

THE MANCELONA VIGILANTE DEBACLE (see page 20) was part of a fairly common phenomenon after a major crime back in the day: Someone holds up a bank and fills up a couple bags of cash, word spreads, citizens grab their guns and form a spontaneous militia. Whether as a sincere desire to help, or for a welcome break from boredom, these rural vigilantes added many hands to tiny sheriff's and police departments across the country. It was kind of a mixed bag, though, as an untrained, heavily armed, impromptu policing force can sometimes get out of control.

Newspaper editorials around the state pointed to the Mancelona mob scene, asking to expand the size of the state police. "It is no more reasonable to expect business men and farmers to become effective, expert police officers over night, than it is to expect police officers to become expert financiers or agriculturists in a day," penned the editorial writers at the *Detroit Free Press*.

But the self-deputized "business men and farmers" liked the posse arrangement, and for good reason. Banks in the 1920s and '30s sometimes paid the ready and willing volunteers after the fact, to make sure they'd be back the next time they heard the alarm. The high incidence of robbery was driving up their insurance rates and other expenses. So on a larger scale, banker associations in Michigan, and several other states, put out the word that they were willing to pay these guns for hire.

Robbery superstar John Dillinger never hit a Michigan bank, and according to some theories, it was because the paid posses were so volatile and scary. It's a relevant point, since he was raised a Hoosier and committed crimes in all three border states and some of them not far from the Michigan state line.

Whether the posse system was a net gain or loss, the Michigan State Police did begin to beef up its force and adopt new technologies (see page 27), discouraging impromptu crime-fighters in favor of better-trained professionals.

In the mid-1920s, two-thirds of the bank robberies in the U.S. were occurring in eight states: Michigan, California, Illinois, Indiana, Kansas, Missouri, Oklahoma and Texas

Port Huron State Police Troops, 1917.
(State of Michigan)

THE ADVENT OF THE MICHIGAN STATE POLICE >>>>>>>>

THE MICHIGAN STATE POLICE WAS BORN IN 1917, after Michigan's and pretty much everyone else's National Guard was called overseas to fight in World War I, leaving the homefront unprotected. That was the kick in the pants that led Michigan to get on the state police force bandwagon with the Texas Rangers, Massachusetts Constabulary and Pennsylvania State Police. That last, ho-hum name, became the norm after it was adopted by Gov. Samuel Pennypacker. Yes. That was his name. Michigan's force was signed into muster by Gov. Albert Sleeper. Not a bad name, either. At first, Michigan's was called the state constabulary, but later fell in line with just about everyone else by adopting the one-size-fits-all "state police" name. Now, everybody has a state police agency, except Hawaii, where each island has its own force.

GOV. SLEEPER WANTS

1—Early ratification dry nation.
2—"Workable" budget law.
3—Extension of highways and creation of highways commission.
4—Uniform accounting.
5—Perpetuation of constabulary.
6—Increased state health powers.
7—Eliminate losing state farms.
8—Supply Michigan people with fish first.
9—Business management for penal institutions.
10—Fire-proof buildings for institutions housing inmates.
11—Salary basis for all sheriffs.
12—Compulsory physical training high schools.
13—To prevent primary election candidates running on two tickets.
14—Foreign languages not to be taught in grade schools.
15—Centralized state printing and purchasing.
16—Reduction of waiting and suspended-payment periods in compensation cases.
17—Increase of maximum and minimum compensation payments.

Lansing State Journal; Jan. 2, 1919.

Michigan State Police fingerprint class. (State of Michigan)

To get started, Michigan recruited the few National Guard members left at home, military veterans and local officers to build a force of 300 troopers; that was about one trooper for every 10,000 residents in the fast-growing state. A lot of them patrolled on horseback, as people were just starting to wrap their heads around the concept of police cars. Or cars in general, for that matter. And while responding to car accidents is now a fairly routine part of the job, in 1918, they attended to a total of only six.

The governor and others intended the Michigan State Constabulary to be a temporary thing, disbanded when the boys came home from over there. But the agency stuck around, partly because of the rampant bootlegging and other Prohibition-related crime in the 1920s and then an outbreak of bank robberies in the 1930s. Even after the FBI took over as the lead investigating and prosecuting agency for bank robbery, the state police and local forces remained the first line of defense after a heist.

The agency's pioneering use of radios in cop cars put them on the cutting edge, even though they were merely one-way communications to begin with. Still, getting the radio directions and updates from headquarters helped them to more quickly catch criminals and respond to emergencies. Notably, the radio system is credited with the quick collaring of two suspects in a Battle Creek robbery and cop killing (see page 71).

And it sure beat the old method of communications: Stopping in at post offices to see if the bosses had sent them a telegram.

EAST LANSING IN HOLLYWOOD

A busy corner of police radio station WRDS at East Lansing, as reconstructed for "Car 99," opening today at the Gladmer, shows Frank Craven, Sir Guy Standing, and Russell Hopton, who are featured with Fred MacMurray and Ann Sheridan in the picture.

Lansing State Journal; Mar 9, 1935.

TROOPERS GO HOLLYWOOD >>>>>>>>

Early on in the history of the Michigan State Police, one of its troopers became the subject of a Hollywood movie. "Car 99" in 1935 starred tall, dimple-chinned Fred MacMurray as a state cop who was a hero for catching several bandits, but then got suspended when he carelessly let a captured bank-robbery gang boss slip through his hands.

When it opened in March of that year, the state police had a "crime doesn't pay" exhibit in the lobby of the Gladmer Theatre in Lansing. In Battle Creek, police handed out movie tickets to people who were seen being courteous to others.

That was more than 80 years ago, though, and the movie and the incident are all but forgotten. So good luck to anyone trying to find the flick online or otherwise.

Still, this wasn't the first time the department was represented in Hollywood. Several mounted Michigan troopers did stunt work for "The Rich Slave," said to be the first commercial movie filmed in the state. The film was released in 1921, and it's apparently even more forgotten than "Car 99".

Bentley Historical Library, University of Michigan

THE U.P.'S BLACK BART

THE YEAR: 1889
THE CRIME: THE LAST STAGE HOLDUP EAST OF THE MISSISSIPPI
THE MOTIVE: A BAD HORSE RIDE AND A LUST FOR DIME-NOVEL FAME

REIMUND HOLZHEY, A 22-YEAR-OLD GERMAN IMMIGRANT WITH TIGHTLY CROPPED HAIR AND A BUSHY MUSTACHE, OBSESSED OVER DIME NOVELS WHILE STAYING IN CHEAP HOTELS IN IRON-MINING COUNTRY.

Before Hollywood began projecting glorified bad-guy images across America, cheap, mass-produced pieces of pop-literature were churned out in New York and dropped off in bundles at whistle-stops all along the westward expansion. Reading was just about the best entertainment to be had. And, just as it is today, romance and murder were the top sellers. And Westerns. In the late 1880s, just a decade after Wounded Knee, the cheap reads pushed the narrative of the brave and noble white man battling blood-thirsty savages to make the prairies safe for farmers and pretty girls. The books mythologized real-life characters like Kit Carson, Billy the Kid, Wild Bill Hickok and Calamity Jane. And there was this guy out in northern California called Black Bart.

Holzhey admired Black Bart, who, as the story goes, had soured on prospecting for gold and took to holding up Wells Fargo stagecoaches. At two of his 28 heists, he sauntered up to a stage on foot (because horses scared him), demanded the loot … and left behind hand-written poems.

He enjoyed about eight years of success, robbing himself a decent living, while reputedly never firing a shot. This peculiar behavior helped groom the legend of the debonair, refined robber.

Our youthful Holzhey would later cultivate that same nickname while skulking around, searching out victims in the iron-filled and increasingly mined bluffs of northern Wisconsin and the Upper Peninsula. Even now, he's sometimes referred to as the Midwestern Black Bart. While that's kind of like being the LeBron James of the rec league, he did match the original in politeness, according to eyewitnesses.

No. 777. Published Every Wednesday. Beadle & Adams, Publishers, 98 WILLIAM STREET, NEW YORK. Ten Cents a Copy. $5.00 a Year. Vol. LX.

BUFFALO BILL'S SPY-SHADOWER

OR,

The Masked Men of Grand Canyon.

A Romance of the Dread Driver of the Colorado.

BY COLONEL PRENTISS INGRAHAM,
AUTHOR OF THE "BUFFALO BILL" NOVELS, ETC.

CHAPTER I.

THE HERMIT OF THE GRAND CANYON.

A HORSEMAN drew rein one morning, upon the brink of what is one of the wonders of the world, yet seen by very few—the Grand Canyon of the Colorado.

A mighty abyss, too vast for the eye to take in in its grand immensity; a mighty mountain rent asunder and forming a chasm which is a valley of grandeur and beauty, through which flows

BUFFALO BILL FOUND A RETREAT UPON THE CLIFF GIVING HIM A VIEW IN BOTH DIRECTIONS.

Still, Holzhey made enough of a splash that his eventual capture was greeted as front-page news in St. Louis and other major cities. Some of the papers seemed to simultaneously build up (or cash in on) his legend, while chastising dime novels for the trashy make-believe that inspired him.

Holzhey's American journey began in Fort Howard, Wisconsin, working at an uncle's sawmill, and then another uncle's gristmill, but as a young man in a strange place, he caught a bad case of wanderlust. He took off for the Pacific northwest, trying his hand at ranching and more mills. He may have heard tall tales of the original Black Bart's exploits around campfires in Washington, Oregon and California. He got a good story of his own when he bounced off a horse and onto his head. He later used the head injury in his defense, claiming he was never a robber

I've labored long and hard for bread,
For honor, and for riches,
But on my corns too long you've tread,
You fine-haired sons of bitches.

Here I lay me down to sleep
To wait the coming morrow,
Perhaps success, perhaps defeat,
And everlasting sorrow.
Let come what will, I'll try it on,
My condition can't be worse;
And if there's money in that box
'Tis munny in my purse.

Poems attributed to Charles Earl Boles, the original Black Bart

before the headaches and evil thoughts that came from the fall. (In fact, a 2017 Harvard study concluded that brain injuries can lead to criminal behavior.)

Holzhey headed back to the Midwest and opened his Black Bart Wisconsin franchise in April, 1889. Though he'd started his life in Schwarzburg, Germany, he went about his crime spree with an un-German-like lack of precision. He started with the hold-up of a stage between Pulcifer and Simonds — shooting a horse and walking away empty handed. His next outing went better: He got a mail pouch with several hundred dollars and $50 from the pockets of the passengers. Then, he robbed a coach on an Indian reservation, and once held up a stage and a train in a single hour. Polite, he may have been, but that was the only trait he shared with his role model. Holzhey was impulsive, disorganized, and more interested in the easiest rather than the most lucrative heist. But his indiscriminate attacks on unlucky wayfarers made him the terror of the area known as the Gogebic (go-GIBB-ic) Iron Range.

The jagged, bouldered shores of cold, deep Lake Gogebic, in the northwest corner of the U.P., became the backdrop of Holzhey's last stand. He chose a coach on its way to the Gogebic station of the Milwaukee, Lake Shore & Western Railroad. Among its four riders were two bankers, one from Minneapolis and one from Montreal — all of them patrons of the White House Inn, a hunting-and-fishing summer resort. Their languid, late-morning ride towards home was disrupted when the desperado sprang from the woods, pointing two pistols at the driver and demanding he "hang on to the reins and don't make a single move at the peril of your life."

But Holzhey misjudged the nature of these town folk — they were hunters, after all — and one of them faked him out by reaching into his pocket, presumably for cash, and drawing his own pistol. He fired on Holzhey and Holzhey shot back. The horses responded frantically, jerking the stage forward. A.C. Fleischbein, a businessman from Belleville, Illinois, chose the wrong time to stand up and took one of the robber's slugs in his hip. It knocked him out of the coach and onto the ground, where he writhed in pain. Holzhey's shots also struck Donald Mackarchar, the Minneapolis banker, in the leg and the side of his head.

Mackarchar would be okay, but as Fleischbein lay bleeding on the ground, Holzhey stuck a gun in his face and pulled $40, a gold watch-and-chain and a ring out of the man's pockets. Then, the robber disappeared back into the hills.

Fleischbein lived long enough to tell the authorities what the highwayman looked like, but he'd lost too much blood waiting on the ground, and even more on the long ride to the hospital in Bessemer, 30 rocky, horse-pulled miles away. He died at the hospital that night.

The death of a well-heeled tourist upped the ante on Holzhey's head. Railroad companies and other businesses offered rewards, totaling more than $6,000 (that's $180,000 in today's dollars, which could change most people's lives).

Holzhey scampered off to Republic, a town southwest of Ishpeming and named for the Republic Iron Company, but his description arrived first. As soon as he paid for a room at the Republic House and signed in as Henry Plant, people noticed that he matched the description of that murderer in Gogebic. While Holzhey got a night's sleep, the hotel owner, a former cop, and some local card players spent the night organizing a small party to grab the suspect in the morning.

Holzhey was allowed a last meal — breakfast at the inn — but when he stepped out for a morning stroll, one of the posse took a shot at him. Holzhey ran and the posse took off after him. He didn't get far before he was tackled. Awash in guilt, he surrendered.

The marshal searched him and found he was carrying several pocketbooks — including one with his own identification papers — as well as three guns and three gold watches. The game was obviously up and the young crook broke down and confessed. Police later found more than 100 dime novels in the room where he lived in Wisconsin, newspapers noted.

While news of Holzhey's capture spread far and wide, it was short-lived and, well, no romantic robber was he. The Black Bart of the Great Lakes was, after all, now a murderer.

Holzhey sobbed when he heard the judge sentence him to a life of "hard labor." In 1893, about three years into his sentence, he volunteered to let doctors cut a hole in his skull to ease pressure on his brain. The theory was that tightness might be causing his headaches, misbehavior and melancholia (what we now call depression). Afterwards, he functioned well enough to be a prison librarian and edit the prisoners' newspaper.

In 1913, Governor Woodbridge Ferris granted him parole. That wasn't anywhere near a life sentence for Holzhey. He worked for years running a photo studio and as a hunting and fishing guide near Marquette. Then, in 1952 — nearly 40 years into his freedom and 63 years after his most infamous crime — he was found in his Ft. Myers, Florida, home with a gun in his hand and another hole in his head. He was 85.

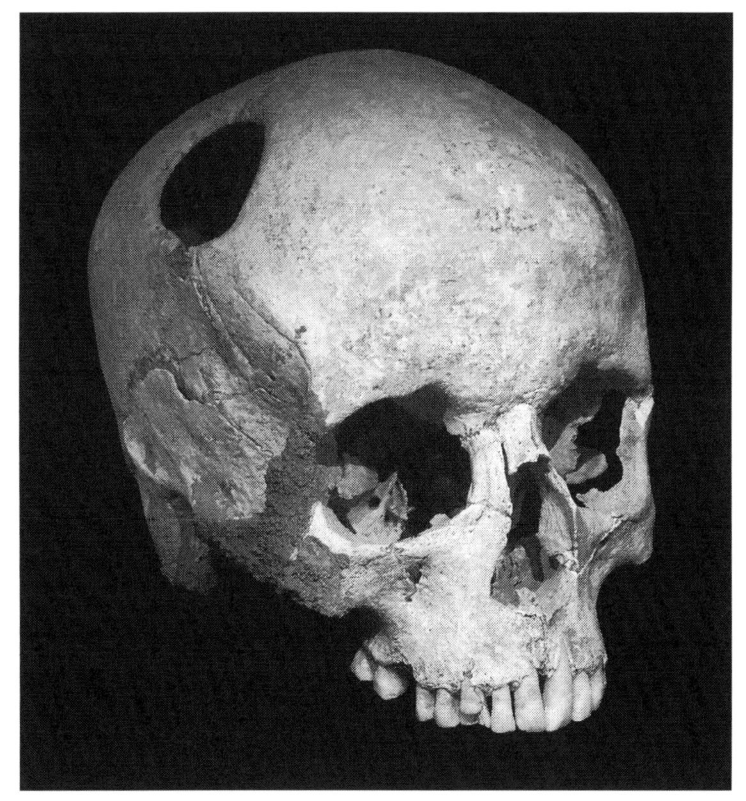

A trepanated Neolithic skull. Notice the rounding off of the hole: This indicates new growth and that the patient survived the operation.

TREPANNING >>>>>>>>

Holzhey repeatedly claimed that he was never a robber before he fell from a horse, resulting in headaches and evil thoughts. When sentenced to the penitentiary, he was reportedly sullen, but not rebellious. When he stole a table knife, however, fashioning it into a stiletto and then holding a guard prisoner for two hours, the warden was forced to shoot him. Rather, he shot at Holzhey's knife hand, shattering four fingers, which were later amputated. Holzhey was later diagnosed as insane and sent to an asylum in Ionia. There, they operated on his skull, lifting a bone that was pressing on his brain. Holzhey returned to Marquette "a changed man" and became the "most trusted man in the prison."

Trepanning — a surgical procedure in which a hole is drilled or scraped into the skull — is, to date, the oldest surgical procedure for which there is archaeological evidence. From 5 - 10% of all Neolithic skulls unearthed around the world show evidence of trepanning. Although ancient cultures probably believed that they were releasing evil spirits through the hole in the skull, trepanning was a precursor to lobotomy and is still sometimes performed today, although under a different term. The procedure is now called a craniotomy.

THE SMALLEYS ROB BIG

THE YEAR: 1895
THE CRIME: TRAIN ROBBERY, COP KILLING
THE MOTIVE: THEY'D GOTTEN AWAY WITH IT BEFORE (THE ROBBERY PART, THAT IS)

JOHN AND ABE SMALLEY GREW UP NORTH OF CLARE WHEN THE WHITE PINES WERE FALLING TO THE CROSS-CUT SAWYERS.

Not much is known about Abe's formative years, but John spent some of his early adulthood working as a lumberer and boxing in local rings, a rough sport for small-time purses.

Legend is that they spent the mid-1880s to mid-1890s burgling stores and farmhouses, as well as pulling off bank and train robberies and dynamiting safes. If that's accurate, they certainly beat the odds of capture far longer than most.

Abe went one step further in lucky escapes, as he claimed to have been part of the bloody 1892 bank raid in Coffeyville, Kansas, that put an end to the Dalton Gang. (The Dalton Gang was led by brothers said to be the second cousins of the even more notorious James Gang.) The story goes like this: Six desperadoes rode in on horseback and simultaneously held up the town's two banks. But the whole town had been tipped off, so as the robbers left the banks with their loot, a barrage of gunfire broke out. Four of the gang were killed, while four townsfolk also fell — a marshal, a bank clerk, a shoemaker and a shop owner. Abe would have been one of the two bandits lucky enough to escape with his skin, though he did take a ball of lead in the small of his back. He later showed off the scar, like a trophy, to his partners in crime.

John, on the other hand, is said to have been nicknamed the "Whiskered Train Robber," though it's unclear how that would have set him apart at a time when bushy moustaches and other big facial hair were not just reserved for hipsters. After all, whole string of presidents from around that time are now better known for their mutton-chops or beards, than for anything they actually did.

GUY LOUIS SELBERT

A photo of the slain members of the Dalton gang hangs in the Dalton Defenders Memorial Museum, along with a few words to the wise.

St. Louis Post Dispatch; Oct. 29, 2000.

John Smalley committed the bulk of his crimes in states other than Michigan, and came home to lead a serene existence on his father's farm, or sometimes in McBain with Cora Brown, a "woman of ill repute" also known as the Black Diamond. Cora was either his wife or his girlfriend, depending on who you ask. Serene or not, law-abiding citizens noticed John's long absences from the area and often speculated how he came by his conspicuous wads of cash.

Cora contributed more than a soft shoulder to the brother's exploits, lending her second cousin James Brown to the Smalleys as they set off on their most infamous score. Two years afterward, Brown penned and signed a vivid confession that contains a lot of what is known about the robbery and escape.

TRAINS WERE THE STATE-OF-THE-ART TRANSPORTATION IN THE POST-CIVIL WAR YEARS. They belched black, sooty clouds as they whistled their way around the ever-growing system of rails, carrying people, mail, cattle, timber, coal and just about anything else that could be sold. And, of course, they also carried money. Trains routinely included what was called an express car, which held the cash to stock the banks and help large companies meet their payrolls. Trains were a popular target for bandits. With normal speeds of only 15 to 20 miles an hour, they were easy to spot and easy to stop.

UNITED STATES OF AMERICA

$1000 $1000

THE LAKE SHORE AND MICHIGAN SOUTHERN RAILWAY COMPANY

1000 1000

No 10473 No 10473

THREE AND ONE-HALF PER CENT. GOLD BOND.

ONE THOUSAND DOLLARS

In Witness whereof

The Lake Shore and Michigan Southern Railway Company has caused these presents to be signed by its President or one of its Vice-Presidents and its corporate seal to be hereunto affixed, and to be attested by its Secretary or an Assistant Secretary and coupons for said interest with the engraved signature of its Treasurer to be attached hereto this first day of June 1897.

The Lake Shore and Michigan Southern Railway Company,

$1000

Gold Bond of the Lake Shore and Michigan Southern Railway Company, issued June 1, 1897.

The Smalley trio had been wandering the area woods, camping, maybe casing a general store or a farmhouse by day. At night, they'd find the least secure entrance, then take the money, watches, food, clothes or whatever they could use. But this was no way to live, and they figured there was a bigger payday for the taking. They decided to make that payday happen about 25 miles south of the Michigan state line near Kendallville, Indiana, at a spot known as the Kessler siding.

The brothers and their new sidekick took cover in a shack near the track where the Lake Shore & Michigan Southern express train out of Chicago was scheduled to pass. Conveniently, there were extra ties and rails stacked nearby, and the three men set about piling them onto the track to block the train. Abe used some of his dynamite to blow the lock off the switch box, and raised the red flag symbol to tell the engineer he'd better put on the brakes.

They waited, seemingly forever, hiding in a shed, checking their stolen pocket watches with the light of a match. They had a schedule and expected the train around 9 or 10, but it was running late. Just shy of midnight on September 12, 1893, they finally heard it chugging out of the distant woods and toward the trap. The brakes tightened on the steel wheels and scraped to a gradual stop. The three bandits, faces half-covered by burgled red handkerchiefs, stepped out from the shadows, pistols drawn. Brown waved a .38 Winchester and Abe threatened with his .44 Smith & Wesson. The trio bounded up the steps and into the engine. Three shots were fired and one hit the engineer by accident. It was later presumed to have been fired by Brown, who was acting on nerves. The wound didn't look like it was going to kill the engineer, and they left him in his pain.

Abe demanded directions to the express car, and the three men gathered around. "Open the door," Abe yelled. The guards and clerks inside refused. Abe had more dynamite and blew open the door. He tossed another stick inside the car for good measure, and when the smoke cleared, John boosted Abe and James inside.

"Hold up your hands," Abe demanded of the railroad employees. "If you do, I won't hurt you."

He asked why there were no lights in the car and a worker replied, "They're blowed out." Abe gave them a match and told them to relight them. He then demanded that they open the safe, but they said they couldn't. It was secured for the trip, and only personnel at the train's destination of Akron, Ohio, had the combination. What about the other "box" safe, Abe asked, but they told him there was nothing in it of value.

Nevertheless, Abe wanted to see for himself and sent Brown to the engine to find the coal hammer. Meanwhile, John Smalley stood outside, along the track, firing off shots from his Winchester every so often to remind the passengers and crew that there was a robbery going on and that they should continue hiding under their seats until further notice. Between shots, he knocked down fences at the bottom of an embankment. That's where they would make their escape, and he hoped it would be soon.

Soon enough, Brown returned with the coal tool and Abe grabbed it to knock a plate off one of the safes. It took three loud, smoky blasts of dynamite to finish the job. The railroad workers, hiding behind boxes, asked if they could hop into another car. Try it, and that guy outside'll shoot you, James Brown told them.

Abe reached into the safe, pulled out four sacks and threw them out of the train and onto the ground. All of this hammering and dynamiting had taken a long time, so the trio rushed to pick up the sacks, then stepped over the fence and into the night. They made their way deep into the woods, heading generally to the north. About half an hour later, they heard the train start up again. Presumably, the crew had removed the rails and ties from the track. It was also a sign of some relief for Brown, who hoped that, maybe, the engineer he'd shot was still alive.

They hiked through the woods until daylight, even doubling back a half mile or so to find Abe's lost handkerchief that would surely tell the sheriff and railroad detectives that the crooks had passed by. When a hard rain began to fall, they stopped, built

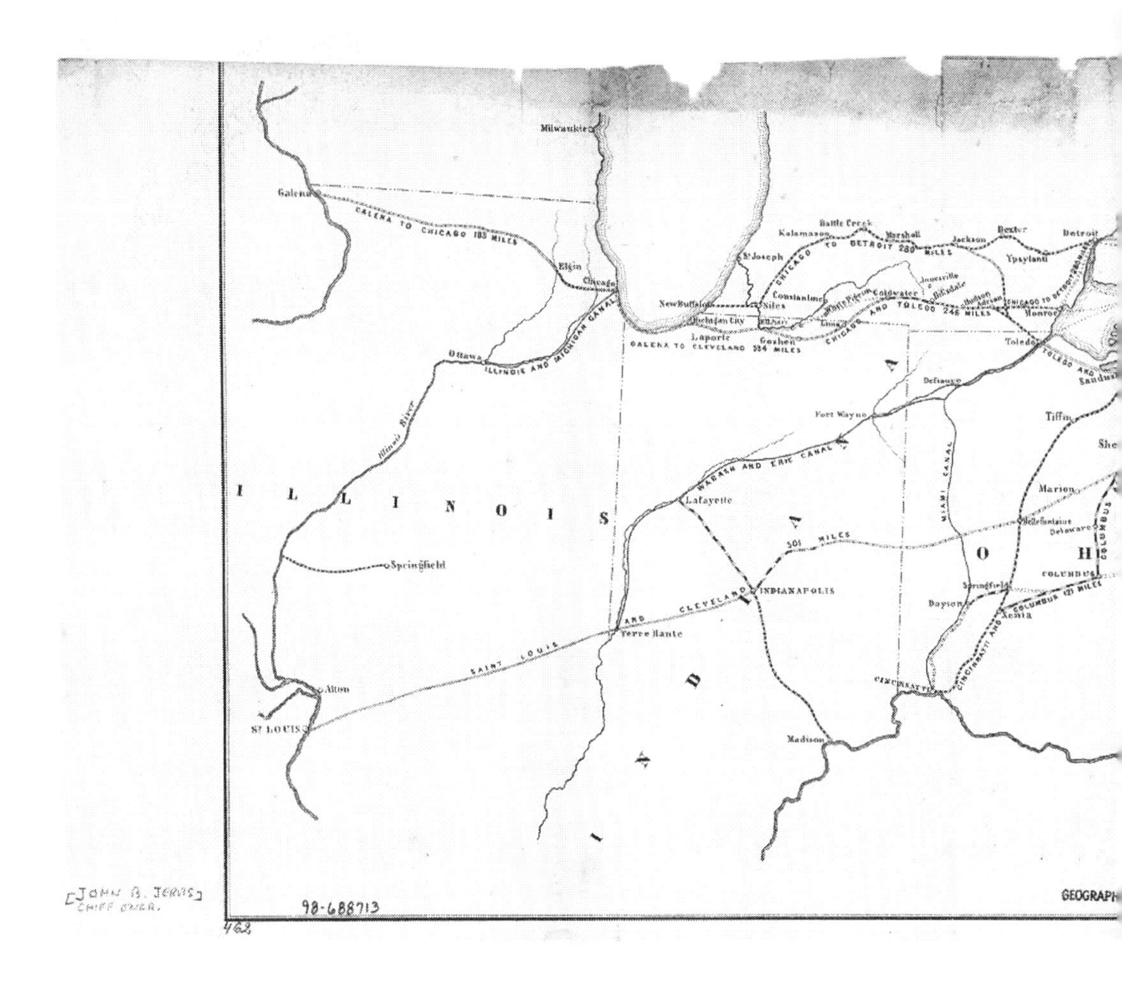

a fire and ate breakfast, finally opening the four sacks to count the loot. They found they'd stolen a whopping $16,000. They'd have to make a haul of more than $400,000 today to equal that in buying power. Each of the men's share was $5,000 and then they drew "cuts"— an archaic term for drawing straws — to see who'd get the extra $1,000. Abe won.

Despite their sudden wealth — or rather because of the way they got it — they kept to the woods for weeks, moving at night and camping out of sight during the day. They were in a hurry to cross the state line; Michigan had abolished the death penalty in 1846, and they figured they'd stand a better chance of avoiding the end of a rope in the Wolverine state. Once across, Abe slunk off, never to be heard from again. James and John continued north toward the center of Michigan.

For 100 miles, they hiked in that clumsy and awkward way until they found themselves in Ionia. The picturesque little city on the banks of the Grand River was already becoming a prison town, with a state men's reformatory and an asylum for the criminally insane. They walked into town separately to freshen up. John Smalley bought a new suit, a gold

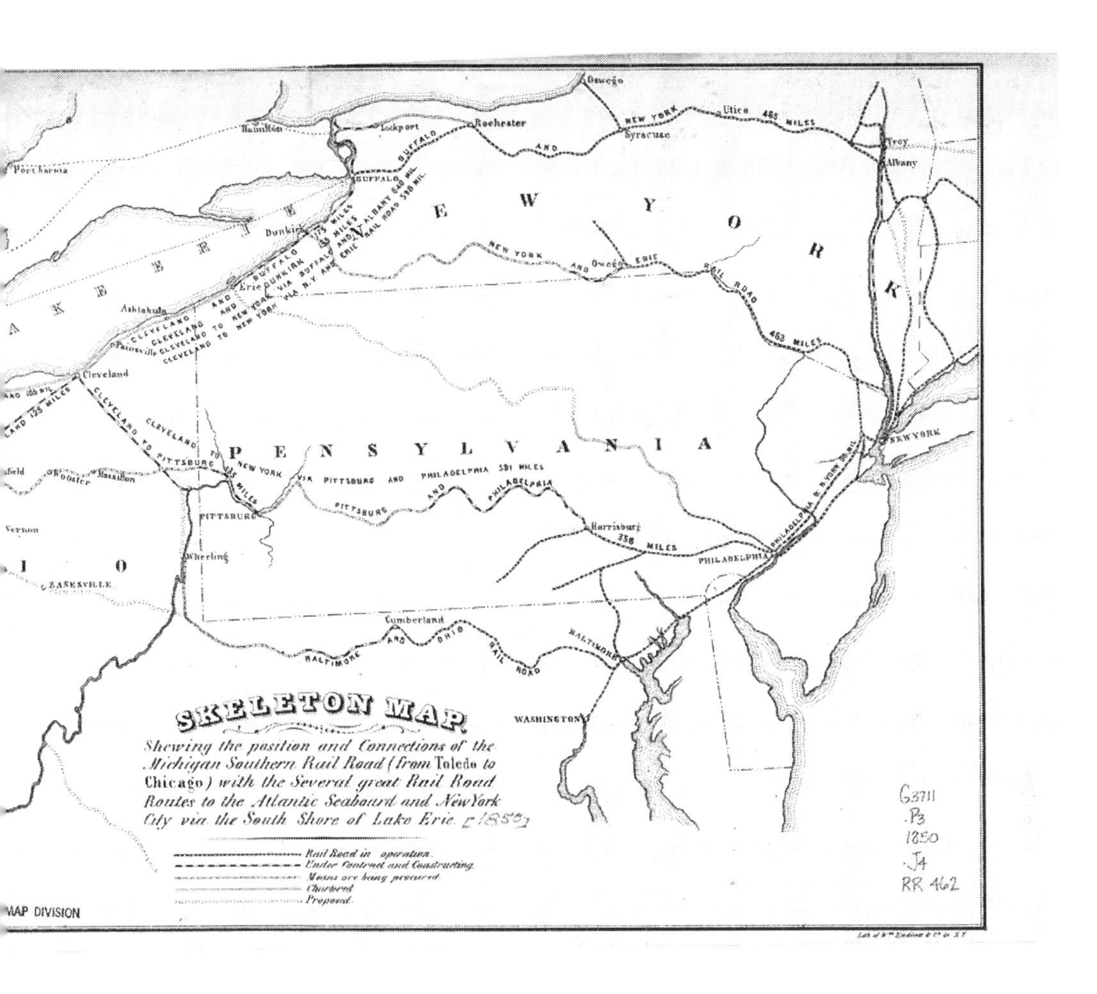

watch and got a little bit drunk. James then went in, sat down for a shave and a haircut and shopped for a change of clothes and a gold watch for his wife.

They'd played it cool in Ionia and nobody there seemed the wiser. Now, they hit the rails again, this time as peaceful, paying passengers. With stops in Edmore, then Alma, and somewhere north of Shepherd, they shook hands on the fortune they'd bagged together. John Smalley hoped his less-experienced accomplice could keep quiet about their score.

James Brown, weighted down by the guilt of the nearly five grand he carried (about $140,000 today), walked the seven miles to Gilmore where his brother-in-law lived. He stayed in the barn. The family knew he was hiding for some good reason and they begrudgingly brought his wife Lena to him. He spilled his guts and told her everything as she wept. Meanwhile, John Smalley went further north to see the family farm and Cora, the Black Diamond.

For the next two years, Smalley hid and spent his cash. James Brown tried to turn down his nagging conscience. All the while, a small legion of detectives from Noble County, Indiana, plus investigators from the bank and the railroad company, looked for clues in the audacious Kendallville train robbery.

IT WAS ABOUT TWO YEARS AFTER THEIR GREAT TRAIN ROBBERY THAT ANOTHER RAILROAD HOLDUP IN SOUTHWESTERN MICHIGAN LED TO JOHN'S DEMISE. In 1895, five bandits stopped a train going past Fennville, near Saugatuck. They filled bags with money belonging to American Express Co., and relieved crew members of their pocket watches and other jewelry. Victims described the apparent ring-leader as having a thick, reddish beard, and one of the accomplices left pointed-toe shoe prints as they fled into the woods.

The city of Grand Rapids was on the lookout, and reports came in of someone matching the description of the ring-leader strolling down Fulton Street. Then police got word of two suspicious characters buying train tickets north of town, heading toward Reed City. While waiting at the depot, witnesses said, they took turns clutching a leather satchel, and one of them pulled out an impressive wad of cash while paying for the tickets.

Just as the Reed City-bound train was making its first stop, a few miles north of town at the Alpine Avenue station, four police officers arrived. They each stepped aboard a different passenger car to search its riders. The conductor signaled to Detective George W. Powers, a Civil War veteran and 18-year member of the Grand Rapids police force, that the suspicious fellow was the guy sitting in the front of the smoking car. Powers climbed the steps and saw a man in a black slouch hat. The detective asked him where he'd boarded. At West Bridge Street, was his reply. The cop asked the man if he was traveling with anyone. The man, peering from under the black hat, pointed across the aisle. A younger man occupied that seat. He wore pointed toe shoes and there was a satchel under his seat. "Is that your grip?" Powers asked, picking up the bag. At that, the older man rose from his seat, pulled out a .44, and shot the officer in the right cheek.

The gunman grabbed the leather bag and bolted out the exit with his partner following close behind. They ran for the cover of the woods A detective and a brakeman ran after them, but they'd gotten too good of a head start. A horse-driven ambulance arrived and took Powers to Butterworth Hospital. Doctors put the comatose officer on the table and looked at how the bullet had torn through his face. They traced the bullet's path to his brain. With late 19th-Century medical technology, they removed the slug, but he died before the sun came up.

The slaying of one of Grand Rapids' finest turned the heat up higher than western Michigan, or the Smalleys, were used to. Posters and handbills asking for clues and other help in capturing the criminals were nailed up all over Grand Rapids and for many miles north. People were eager to help, and several whiskered men going about their business were temporarily pegged as suspects.

But the big break came when the leaflets made their way to the bustling sawmill and railroad town of Cadillac. That's about 20 miles from McBain, and Cora's house, where John Smalley had shown up again, just recently. His long and lucrative absences were about to catch up with him. Some of his neighbors speculated that the reddish-haired gent who sometimes lived among them may have just shaved off a reddish beard to throw off any comparisons. Someone passed along those suspicions, along with Smalley's favorite haunts, to Deputy Bert Spafford and ex-Sheriff Gillis McBain. They gathered up repeating Winchester rifles and a small posse, and snuck over to Cora Brown's house. As dusk settled in, the people in the house lit lanterns and their yellow, wavy light was enough for the hunting party to recognize John Smalley. He was sitting in a rocking chair, chatting with the others.

The two men who actually had badges motioned for their vigilantes to hang back while they crept up to the porch. As their boots eased onto the first wooden steps, Smalley thought he heard something. He stood up and opened the door just a crack. There were two men with rifles looking right at him. He slammed the door shut and turned to take cover as Cora and her other guests bolted out the back door. McBain and Spafford opened fire at the door and two shots splintered through and into the flesh of the fugitive, one lodging in his neck.

But the lawmen weren't sure if he'd been hit or had fled out the back with the rest of them. They didn't want to assume anything, so they waited an hour before easing into the home — and there lay Smalley, dead, his blood oozing out and staining the floor.

Police brought witnesses from Fennville and Grand Rapids to confirm John Smalley's identity, though the body was rapidly turning ripe in the late August heat. Consensus was that, yes, this was one of the guys who held up the train and shot the policeman. Still, there were those, both in the law and in public, who believe they'd gotten it wrong, and doubts remain 120-plus years later. One popular theory is that Abe Smalley was the one who pulled off Fennville, and the one who murdered Powers. Some believe his accomplice in pointy footwear was John's 19-year-old son, Oscar. Police interrogated Oscar, but were never able to build a case against him. According to some, Abe fled to the Southwest. If it was him, this time, he disappeared for good.

The only one of the surviving bunch who ever faced justice was James Brown, who, after being found out by a railroad detective, turned over the remaining $1,500 of his Kendallville take and was taken to Allegan County Jail. After he penned his lengthy confession, he was sent to Indiana to face trial.

BURIED BOOTY >>>>>>>>

JOHN SMALLEY IS THOUGHT TO HAVE BEEN A PROLIFIC TRAIN ROBBER. SOME HAVE PLACED HIS CRIMINAL TAKINGS AT A WHOPPING $1 MILLION. IF TRUE, AND IF THAT'S IN 1895 DOLLARS, THAT WOULD BE LIKE $28 MILLION TODAY.

That may be inflated, but he still stole a lot of loot that wasn't recovered after his death. So what happened to all of it? That's a question that's been asked by several people around the McBain area, and it's never been answered. A popular theory is that he divided up the money and buried it in holes around Clare, McBain and Falmouth.

There are many other caches of treasure rumored to be buried in Michigan soil. Not all of them are the results of robbery or other shady dealings. Some are from misers who simply wanted to hide their riches in places other than banks and safes. There's no way to know for sure if all of these deposits by shovel really do exist, unless someone actually finds them. Also, while the locations listed are pretty general, they're about as precise as possible. But then, hey, if the exact locations were known, someone would have already dug them up.

Here are some of them, according to local lore:

BROHMAN — 1874: A gang held up a stagecoach carrying $74,000 (a half million today) in gold to a lumber camp near Baldwin. One of the bad guys is said to have buried it in an iron stove and it's believed to still be there, west of Brohman on the north shore of Benton Lake. Two tree stumps marked the spot at the time, but then, tree stumps rot.

GRASS LAKE — 1920: On July 29, a gang of fishermen robbed the Farmers State Bank in the village of Grass Lake, about 10 miles east of Jackson. Despite a gunfight that broke out as they fled, they got away. They're said to have buried some of the loot on an island in a small lake. The question is, which island? The village is on a lake of the same name, and the smaller Tims Lake, just north, also has a prominent island. There are several other small lakes in the area (this is Michigan, after all), so a survey of how many of them have islands might be in order. The crooks got away with about $1,000 in gold, and that's in 1920 values. One grand in cash then would be around $13,000 now, but gold prices have fluctuated widely in the past century. However much that comes out to, it would be a pretty good take for a walk around a lake with a metal detector.

BRANCH AND HILLSDALE COUNTIES — 1860s: Silas "Sile" Doty was a prolific inter-state robber, originally from Vermont. He started his thievery in New England and when the law was on his tail, he sailed to Old England and outlawed for a couple years in Liverpool, London and Scotland. When he figured it was safe, he returned to the eastern U.S. and picked up where he'd left off. He made too big of a name for himself there again so, in 1834, he and his wife made their way to Adrian, in the Michigan Territory, three years before statehood.

He continued his life of crime here and in Ohio, Indiana and Illinois. To his credit, sort of, he helped a slave escape from Kentucky to Ohio, though his motive is said to have been more for the adventure of it than any opposition to slavery.

It wasn't just robbery that filled up his criminal resume. He moved for a time to northern Indiana, where he beat to death a hired farm hand who'd threatened to turn him in to the law. Later, he was jailed in Virginia (in a part that's now West Virginia) for stealing horses, but escaped with the help of tools smuggled in by a friend.

As a trained blacksmith, he often made his own skeleton keys and other lock-picking tools he used in his real trade, robbery/burglary. Other tricks up his sleeve included feeding poisoned meat to watchdogs; or stealing a getaway horse, and having an associate gallop away on a different mount in the opposite direction, to confuse any pursuers.

He had a long career, and during the Civil War, he's said to have taken advantage of the fact that so many men had gone south and east to fight, making for easier pickin's in the North. He did stints in jails in Michigan and Indiana, as well, and continued to rob and burgle into his 70s, when he died of pneumonia at a son's home in Reading, just a few miles north of both the Indiana and Ohio borders. He is said to have buried much of his takings in that south central region of the state. There's also a cave called Silas Doty Cave in Hillsdale County, where he reputedly hid stolen horses. The cave is near the North Country Trail.

FAYETTE — 1800s: Alphonse Berlanquette was a saloon owner, who ran a bar just around a bend of beach from Fayette on the Garden Peninsula. As Fayette became a dry town and Berlanquette's was the only watering hole within staggering distance, it grew into a popular and likely lucrative business. Yet Berlanquette was notoriously miserly, and never spent more of his considerable profits than was necessary. He also didn't trust banks. So legend has it that he stashed his wealth in the sandy soil, in the woods, or perhaps a cave in the area of the short-lived, late 1800s industrial settlement.

After he died, his widow tried to find the hidden loot, as did several treasure seekers. Nobody is known to have ever uncovered a cent of it. Later, Berlanquette's relatively respectable establishment came under the ownership of Jim Summers, a notorious kidnapper and pimp (see page 76).

HIGH ISLAND AND BENTON HARBOR — MID 19TH AND EARLY 20TH CENTURIES:

High Island is in the northern end of Lake Michigan, while Benton Harbor is at the southern end. Still, they are both possible sites of treasures left there by offbeat, 19th and 20th Century religious sects.

High Island, which is four miles west of the larger Beaver Island, may hold treasures of both groups. The island, which is now a wildlife research area for the state Department of Natural Resources, may have been the depository for the House of David and of Beaver Island's self-crowned king, James Jesse Strang.

King Strang was shot in 1856, after claiming the island for his Mormon offshoot band of followers. The kingdom's treasury was built up partly by operating a fueling stop for ships, and partly by pirates raiding passing vessels (see page 47). As the king lay dying, legend has it that a follower buried many of the accrued valuables on High Island's northeast side. Unfortunately, a tree that had helped mark its location fell later that century when lumber companies swept through the island.

"BEARDED BABE RUTH": Thomas Dewhirst, shown here in his prime, was known as the "Bearded Babe Ruth" of the House of David baseball team. One year he hit 38 home runs. And he batted over .400 for three consecutive seasons. Dewhirst, who also managed the team for several years, says his top thrill was playing an exhibition game in New York's Polo Grounds, former home of the New York Giants.

The Herald Palladium; Jul 11, 1978.

Then, from 1912 to 1927, the House of David, another cult based in Benton Harbor and well-known for its baseball team, had a colony on the island where about 150 of its members grew potatoes and other food for the vegetarian sect. As the order thrived, the leader, Benjamin Purnell, is said to have parlayed his religious teachings into millions of dollars in wealth. After a sex scandal brought him down, the riches were never accounted for. Some have speculated that they were buried on High Island, while others believed they may be hidden near the group's Diamond Mansion in Benton Harbor.

PIRATES FOR THE KING

THE YEAR: 1850s
THE CRIME: TREACHERY ON THE FRESHWATER SEAS
THE MOTIVE: BUILDING A KINGDOM

"KING" JAMES STRANG'S INFAMOUS BAND OF 500 OR SO MORMON-OFFSHOOT FOLLOWERS WERE RUN OUT OF NAUVOO, ILLINOIS; GREEN BAY, WISCONSIN; AND AT LEAST THREE OTHER TOWNS BEFORE TAKING OVER BEAVER ISLAND AND RUNNING OUT THE LOCAL SETTLERS AND FISHERMEN.

Strang was a religious cult leader and self-dubbed royal with four wives. When he wasn't bullying the islanders, he was in Lansing, casting votes as a state legislator. Meanwhile, pirates robbed passing ships to build up his kingdom's treasury.

Cargo vessels and their crews disappeared mysteriously around the island at that time and many believed Strang's pirates boarded them, killed the crews, took the cargo and burned the ships at sea. Strangites were said to have employed a crooked lighthouse keeper who also lured ships onto the rocks for his highness's buccaneers to pick clean. And the pirates didn't just wait for their prey to sail by. They also took to the lake and went ashore in port towns to rob and pillage stores and warehouses.

After Strang was killed by two disgruntled subjects, his followers awaited divine instruction on his successor, as he had taught them to do. Meanwhile, several Strangites were arrested for crimes and faced trial on the mainland. Eventually, the people who had been banished from the island — and others who didn't like what they'd heard about the Strangites — sailed to the island and rounded up and beat the 1,600 or so members. They boarded them on boats and pushed them out onto Lake Michigan to fend for themselves. Thus was the island re-inhabited by those the Strangites called "gentiles."

In years since, shipwrecks have been found offshore of the island and skeletons were found buried on the island — many of both attributed to the marauding pirates.

CALICO JACK >>>>>>>>

Calico Jack, who gained notoriety as a pirate of the Caribbean despite his fabric-based nickname, is believed to have gotten his start in the Great Lakes. He stole fishing tackle, boats and other valuables around the shores of the lakes in the early 1700s. That was about the time Antoine de la mothe Cadillac established Fort Ponchartrain to trade with and take advantage of the native Chippewa, Huron, Ottawa, Potawatomi and other tribes. (The fort would change and grow into the city of Detroit, and Cadillac would gain greater fame some 200 years later as a car.)

A GENERAL

HISTORY

OF THE

PYRATES,

FROM

Their firſt RISE and SETTLEMENT in the Iſland of *Providence*, to the preſent Time.

With the remarkable Actions and Adventures of the two Female Pyrates

MARY READ and ANNE BONNY;

Contain'd in the following Chapters,

Introduction.
Chap. I. Of Capt. *Avery*.
II. Of Capt. *Martel*.
III. Of Capt. *Teach*.
IV. Of Capt. *Bonnet*.
V. Of Capt. *England*.
VI. Of Capt. *Vane*.
VII. Of Capt. *Rackam*.
VIII. Of Capt. *Davis*.
IX. Of Capt. *Roberts*.
X. Of Capt. *Anſtis*.
XI. Of Capt. *Worley*.
XII. Of Capt. *Lowther*.
XIII. Of Capt. *Low*.
XIV. Of Capt. *Evans*.
XV. Of Capt. *Phillips*.
XVI. Of Capt. *Spriggs*.
And their ſeveral Crews.

To which is added.

A ſhort ABSTRACT of the Statute and Civil Law, in Relation to Pyracy.

The ſecond EDITION, with conſiderable ADDITIONS

By Captain CHARLES JOHNSON.

LONDON:

Printed for, and ſold by *T. Warner*, at the *Black-Boy* in *Pater-Noſter-Row*, 1724.

Top: Anne Bonny, 1697 – 1720.

Right: Published in 1724, "A General History of the Pyrates" is the source of most popular legends. The author used a pseudonym and is to this day unknown.

We don't know a lot about his Great Lakes exploits, but he sailed out of the St. Lawrence Seaway and down to Jamaica, where he continued his pirating ways. Eventually, the law, or what passed for the law, caught up with him and hanged him in 1720 along with several other pirates.

Born in England as John Rackham, Jack was not the most successful or famous pirate, but he gained fame for a couple of things. First, he was ahead of his time for accepting two women on his crew. One was Anne Bonny. She was married to another pirate when she and Jack fell in love; the two stole a vessel to escape the jilted husband's wrath. Mary Read, the other woman on his crew, first hopped on pirate ships dressed as a man. Jack is also, reputedly, the first pirate captain to sail under the flag with a skull over crossbones or two crossed swords, known as the Jolly Roger. His first mate, Karl Starling, is credited with designing the flag.

The Great Lakes has seen many pirates throughout the years, as ships full of furs, timber, liquor and other valuables have been too great a temptation for the criminally inclined. Most of Michigan's buccaneers are forgotten, though those who made a splash in lasting infamy are the crews of King James Jesse Strang (see page 47); and Dan Seavey, who ran ships aground on Lake Michigan in the early 20th Century with fake navigation lights and sank a rival's vessel and crew with a cannon. He was charged with piracy but acquitted.

SELFIE INCRIMINATION

THE YEAR: 2014

THE CRIME: BANK ROBBERY/MODERN VANITY

THE MOTIVE: A LUST FOR MONEY AND FACEBOOK LIKES

WE'VE ALL HEARD ABOUT PEOPLE WHO'VE DESTROYED THEIR CAREERS WITH CARELESS FACEBOOK POSTS. WELL, IT CAN WRECK A CRIMINAL CAREER, TOO.

Brooklyn, New York, transplant Jules Bahler stole about $15,000 from three banks in Bay City and Pontiac in February and March, 2014. In the Pontiac crimes, he presented a note to a teller, but in the Bay City job, the last of the three, he carried a Norinco semi-automatic handgun with an extended barrel.

The day after the Bay City robbery, the FBI found out about his Facebook page, on which he identified himself as King Romeo. He'd posted a selfie that matched surveillance camera shots of him from the banks, as well as the gun, which matched descriptions from witnesses of the Bay City holdup.

He also typed in his feed "Bought my first house And chopper today … lifes great."

In case he hadn't done enough investigators' work for them, he posted a picture of the home in which he was staying in Pontiac. Police performed a stakeout, and when he got in a car driven by a friend, they followed the car and pulled it over. The officers arrested Bahler and found a duffel bag in the car containing a submachine gun.

Social media has helped law enforcement throughout the country on several occasions. Vandals, drug users, jail escapees and even murderers have been caught on several occasions after posting words and photos that either stupidly boasted of crimes or carelessly provided clues.

Bahler, who had been a member of a gang known as the Latin Kings, confessed and pleaded guilty. He was sent to prison for up to 10 years.

FLINT TEACHER BREAKS BAD

THE YEAR: 2003
THE CRIME: ROBBERY BY BOMB SCARE
THE MOTIVE: DOING A DRUG DEALER'S BIDDING

TERESA M. BAIRD'S BANK ROBBING CAREER BEGAN AT 5:20 P.M., MARCH 24, 2003, WHEN SHE WALKED UP TO A DRIVE-THROUGH WINDOW OF CITIZENS BANK IN GENESSEE TOWNSHIP WEARING A CAP WITH THE CARTOON CHARACTER TWEETY BIRD DEPICTED ON IT AND A HEADSET CELL PHONE. Crying, she gave a note to the teller. The note said the bank would blow up in five minutes, unless the teller gave her cash. While she muttered into the headset here and there, she told the bank worker that she was talking to the person who could detonate the bomb at any time.

A month later, when she robbed a National City Bank in Clio, her note included an apology and stated that two men with guns "made me do this." Police jumped to the conclusion that this was the same robber who pulled off the Genessee job, the suspect they'd been referring to as the Tweety Bird robber.

She struck again. And again. Police believed she'd robbed seven times before the end of the year, hitting banks in the Flint area — the farthest from there being a bank in Lapeer — pocketing about $18,000 in her unarmed, but threatening, heists. That's the equivalent of more than $24,000 now. Her nervousness seemed to subside with experience.

Three days before Christmas, she walked into a Citizens Bank branch on West Vienna Road, handed the teller a note and walked out with the cash. (Incidentally, she had already robbed that branch in August.) Like most serial criminals, she eventually slipped up, but in this case it's kind of a head-scratcher.

After the usual threatening note and pay-off, she was seen taping the robbery note over the license plate of her burgundy, 1999, Pontiac Bonneville. Presumably, she didn't want anyone to identify the car by the plate. Yet, as it's illegal to drive around with a hidden plate, a police officer pulled her over. He removed the note, saw what it was, then searched the car and found the money from her latest heist.

X

Then came the big surprise. Police named Baird, a fifth-grade teacher at Washington Elementary School, well-liked and with a spotless work record, as the Tweety Bird Robber.

Teachers don't make a lot of money, but still, nobody could figure out why she'd jeopardize her career this way. Perhaps it was the recent death of her father and the emotional strain of it, some speculated. Her lawyer requested a mental fitness exam for her, which the judge granted. Some theorized that she suffered from multiple personalities.

Later, she said it was because she had become involved with a marijuana dealer who had threatened her with stealing some of his merchandise. She turned to robbery to pay him off and to protect her family.

She was sentenced from 2 to 20 years in prison.

>>>>>>>>

CAUGHT RED-HANDED (LITERALLY) ANTI-BANK ROBBERY TECHNOLOGY

One of the better-known technologies employed to thwart bank robberies is the exploding dye pack. Many U.S. banks have them ready for a teller to slip into a bank bag if someone points a gun at his or her face. A timer detonates the device, hidden in a hollowed out stack of bills. If all goes as planned, the red or purple dye, extremely difficult to remove, will mark the robber for easy identification and render the moolah unspendable. Hollowed out bands of bills might also conceal an electronic tracking device to allow police to locate it through global positioning system (GPS) tracking.

If the thief's money bag doesn't contain a dye pack or a tracking device, it may include a far subtler trap, known as "bait money." That refers to banded bundles that are set aside just in case of a robbery. The serial numbers of all the bills in the bundle are recorded by the bank, making it easier to trace when the money is spent. Presumably, a crook won't know which of the bundles is bait.

Of course, security cameras are everywhere, and have been for quite some time. Still, when TV runs a picture of a suspect taken from one of them, the resolution often looks worse than Civil War-era photos and it seems a wonder that the images ever result in an arrest. But many banks are getting better cameras that are said to take actually recognizable pictures of people.

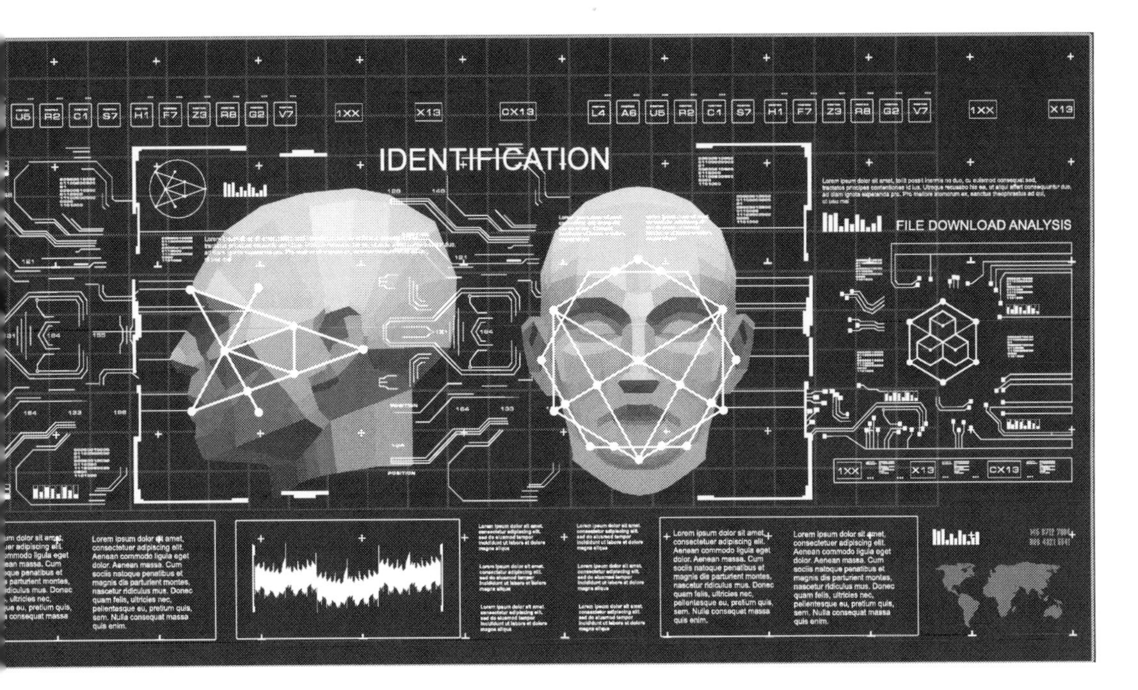

Facial recognition technology has also been used to identify suspects in bank robberies. A combination of tips from surveillance video and of facial recognition tech helped police arrest Kenneth Ardis in Mount Clemens for robbing Talmer Bank and Trust in 2016. Obviously, a mask can thwart a surveillance camera or face I.D., but walking into a bank with a mask is going to put everyone on their guard right from the start.

While the technology is being steadily refined, it's had some disastrous screw-ups in recent years. A man in Denver, Colorado, was arrested in 2014 as a bank robbery suspect due to false identification by the technology. He was acquitted after they determined they'd gotten it wrong. A year later, he was arrested again based on the same technology. He later sued, saying the two false arrests had ruined his career and his marriage.

Silent alarms have also been around for quite some time. The way it works is that a teller pushes a hidden button, notifying police. Hopefully, they make it there in time to grab the suspect. These days, the initial signal often goes to the bank's contracted security company, which then calls the police. Problems sometimes arise when the security company is located hundreds of miles away. With that often cumbersome process, the results of silent alarms have been mixed.

Cell phones have also been tracked to find crooks, though police must first have an idea of the suspect's identity. The cell phone data can then be used to track the movements of the criminal. That generally involves a court order and/or the cooperation of the cell phone company. This is controversial because it often involves law enforcement having access to phone-tracking data of thousands of law-abiding citizens in addition to that of the suspect.

A less common method of security is a "man trap" door, in which there are two sets of doors at a bank's entrance. The second door may require identification before opening. In an even higher-tech version, a metal detector may search for weapons before entry into the second door is allowed.

A bank may employ one or several of the methods, and unless a robber has done a good job of casing the joint, he or she will likely not know which methods are being used in the institution of choice.

Yet none of the efforts so far are fool-proof, since, well, banks are still being robbed.

THE ZIPLOC BANDIT

THE YEAR: 2002 – 2005
THE CRIME: ARMED (APPARENTLY) ROBBERY
THE MOTIVE: IT'S BEEN WORKING SO FA·R

DANIEL W. ARMSTRONG WAS A SUCCESSFUL BANK ROBBER FOR THE THREE YEARS HIS LUCK LASTED.

From 2002 to 2005, a man wearing sunglasses and a bandanna robbed 19 different banks, starting in Port Huron, spreading south to the Flint area and ending up in Livonia. He would stride into the bank lobbies armed with a gun and Ziploc plastic bags and order everyone down on the floor. He'd hand the bags to the tellers and ask them to fill 'em up with fifties and hundreds, and then get out fast.

He never fired a shot in the terrifying hold-ups and police finally found out that he couldn't have if he'd wanted to.

On February 1, 2005, he walked into a Standard Federal bank in Livonia and repeated the formula that had worked so well for him, walking out with $7,000. But this time, the police were not far behind. They collared him, cuffed him and found out the gun he'd been wielding was a fake.

Still, that was enough to slap him with a charge of using a firearm in the commission of a crime, on top of the robbery charges.

BY THE NUMBERS >>>>>>>

Among other things the Feds tell us about bank robbers is that most of them like to work early in the business day. The most popular time to rob a bank is between 9 and 11 a.m.

They also like to start their weekends off with a bang, since Friday is the most popular day of the week to ply their trade. Guess that means bank tellers might not be quite as TGIF as the rest of us.

BABY FACE NELSON

AND THE GETAWAY THAT GOT AWAY

THE YEAR: 1933
THE CRIME: BANK ROBBERY BY GANG
THE MOTIVE: MONEY AND REPUTATION

THE CAST OF CHARACTERS FOR THE PEOPLE'S SAVINGS BANK OF GRAND HAVEN: FIRST, BABY FACE NELSON, A FEISTY CRIMINAL WHO WOULD LATER BECOME PUBLIC ENEMY NUMBER ONE. Then there was his sidekick, Eddie Bentz, a quieter and more cerebral brand of criminal, who should have been Baby Face's boss. Nelson was the crime mastermind and it was nearly a fiasco.

George "Baby Face" Nelson is said to have gotten his infamous nickname when victims and witnesses described the 5-foot-4 bandit as looking like a kid. It's said that the guy born as Lester Joseph Gillis didn't care for the moniker, though it probably sounded at least as tough as Lester Joseph Gillis. He'd devoted his life to being an imposing thug, and he took on the alias George Nelson as a criminal. So instead of George "Baby Face" Nelson, perhaps he should be referred to as Lester Joseph "George 'Baby Face' Nelson" Gillis.

He of the infantile countenance was 24 and already an ex-con before the career-turning Grand Haven job. At a young age, he'd busied himself with home burglaries, street muggings and auto theft. He'd worked for the illustrious Al Capone and served a year in the Illinois state pen at Joliet, for robbing a bank in Chicago. He'd also crafted a reputation for a volatile temper and being cocky enough to burgle the jewelry of some of Chicago's richest and most powerful. After he stood trial for a robbery in Wheaton, Illinois, he escaped during transport and bolted to Reno, Nevada, and then to California, where he worked as a guard for liquor smugglers.

Eventually, he decided he wanted to break into the business of big-time bank scores. His neighbor in Michigan City, Indiana, at the time was Alvin Karpis, a prolific bank robber in the Midwest who went by the name "Creepy Karpis." More than happy to help out, Karpis hooked the eager crook up with Eddie Bentz.

Bentz was a methodical, organized robber who's said to have bagged a million bucks or more in his career. That'd be like $18 million-plus, now. Bank robbers changed partners more often than jazz musicians in those days, and Bentz had jammed with the likes of Machine Gun Kelly, the well-known robber, bootlegger and kidnapper from Memphis, Tennessee. He was known to visit banks posing as a wealthy depositor in order to see their security measures and floor layout. The bankers never suspected that he was only interested in making a withdrawal.

For this upcoming job, he wanted to be the driver. Now the role of chauffeur on a job is kind of like the Ringo of the gang-heist world. It's easily overlooked, but of utmost importance. The crooks who trivialized did so at their peril. They were the ones who were more likely to end up living where the toilets are right next to the beds. Bentz knew that, and wanted it to be his task in this caper.

He figured he'd set about it with his usual studiousness and precision. Like casing the bank itself, he'd find gravel roads and two-tracks that weren't even on the map. You never know when you may have to cut sharp onto a farmer's lane and zip through an orchard or get lost in the woods. The key was to get away fast, and know where you'll end up if you have to make a quick turn.

But Nelson insisted that he needed Bentz's cool head and expertise inside the bank with the other gun-toters. So they ended up hiring a driver now known only as Freddie.

IT WAS THE TAIL-END OF THE SUMMER CABIN SEASON AND GRAND HAVEN WAS DOING THAT LATE SUMMER AFTERNOON MOSEY. Just before 3 p.m., a Buick piloted by Freddie pulled up to the front of the bank on Washington Street at Third. The diminutive Nelson was the first to stroll into the bank, carrying a basket. He handed teller Art Welling $20, asking for change in coins.

As Welling settled into the tedium of counting out change, Nelson pulled a Tommy gun out of the basket. Three other gunmen, including Bentz, stepped up to work the other windows. Then Bentz ordered them to let him to the vault.

Welling was handing over the money just as the man with a boy's face and a gun had told him. He was also, discreetly, stepping on a silent alarm. It rang into the police station and the furniture store next door. The owner of that store, Edward Kinkema (who was also in the undertaking business) grabbed his Remington repeater shotgun and headed out to seek other recruits to help bust up the robbing party.

Kinkema spotted what was obviously the getaway car, manned and idling next to the bank. He stuck his gun in the window, point-blank at the driver. Gambling that the furniture-cum-coffin seller wouldn't blast his head full of shot pellets right then and there, the driver put the car in gear and screeched away and out of town. As word got out about what was going on behind the bank's blinds — drawn down by the robbers when the stickup began — pedestrians fled, while a growing throng of armed citizens took up positions to take their chance at becoming heroes. When the thugs appeared on the street with their loot, they shielded themselves with bank workers, holding them close to absorb any potential high-velocity lead chunks.

The doorways and alleys were filling up with citizens squinting their eyes and training their rifles. Those who didn't have a gun bolted for a covered perch to peek safely at the action. The robbers scanned the block and the vigilante mob. They didn't see the one thing they were looking for: the getaway car. No Buick. No Freddie.

As the bullets began to zip around them, they let go of the captives, returned fire and ran. Kinkema and his cousin grabbed one of the robbers in the Third Street alley and wrestled him to the gravel-strewn ground. Kinkema either felt merciful or he didn't need to drum up any extra business for the funeral-home end of his enterprise; he used his long-gun's butt instead of its trigger. He reared it back and slammed its curvey stock right into the bandit's skull. That'll dim one's prospects, at the very least for an afternoon. Just to make sure, he grabbed the robber's pistol and shot him in the hand. An ambulance picked him up and took him straight to the Ottawa County Jail. Harry Harris was the name he gave his captors as the on-call doctors tended to his wounds.

Harry's accomplices hoofed it to an intersection, cursing absent Freddie's name and his life. That's when they spotted an idling Chevy with two women, a baby and four children in it. They told the moms and kids to get the hell out. The driver — her baby on the seat next to her — clutched the wheel and refused. The other mother grabbed her four children without comment; she figured that a quick am-scray was the best way out. Meanwhile, a suited man with a gun grabbed driver mom and yanked her out of the car. Two arms handed the baby out the window just before the car screeched away with Nelson, Bentz and company. (In one version of the story, the gangsters actually considered taking the baby to keep anyone from shooting at them. If so, cooler heads thankfully prevailed. And really, even armed robbers don't need that kind of publicity.)

The Chevrolet got them out of town for a little breathing room, but it didn't get them anywhere near their destination, the Indiana state line. They rounded Holland and had kicked up some sand a few miles south when somebody looked at the gas gauge. The needle was bouncing on "E." This jalopy clearly wasn't going to get them back to Indiana unless they wanted to pull up to a gas station… No, the other side of that boundary was where they needed to be. Any Michigan cops on their tail would have to slam on the brakes at the first foot of Hoosier highway because bank robbery was still a state crime.

Al Capone, Public Enemy No. 1, with his mother.

Baby Face Nelson, Public Enemy No. 1, 1934.

MORE PRECIOUS THAN LIFE >>>>>>>>

In 1934, President Franklin Roosevelt made bank robbery a federal crime. It was becoming way too common. And while a lot of bank robberies end in murder, it wasn't the killing that got Washington's attention. This wasn't human life they were worried about. This was important. This was money.

It also set the stage for the legendary showdown between young J. Edgar Hoover's FBI and the punks stealing the Federal Reserve Notes. And it cleared the way for the string of bloody endings for Dillinger, Nelson, Floyd, Parker/Barrow, and other Depression-era enemies of the banking community.

HOW MUCH? >>>>>>>>

Why the differences in amounts reported stolen in robberies?

Newspapers often reported wildly different amounts taken in a single bank robbery, particularly in the crime's heyday of the 1930s. Reasons for the discrepancies are hard to determine, though the amounts taken might be understated in early reports, as banks may have wanted to discourage copycats.

Grand Haven Thug In Jackson Prison

EARL DOYLE

GRAND HAVEN, Sept. 11 (AP)—His sentencing and transfer marked by almost unprecedented secrecy, Earl Doyle, 35-year-old Chicago and Kansas City gunman, was starting a life sentence in the Jackson state prison Monday for his part in the $4,000 robbery of the Peoples Savings bank here August 18.

With only the attorneys, court officers, the judge and the defendant present, Judge Fred T. Miles accepted Doyle's plea of guilty late Saturday night and pronounced sentence.

Lansing State Journal; Sep 11, 1933.

Lucky for them, they spotted a blue Chrysler Imperial parked on the side of U.S. 31. The sleek, long-hooded sedan would have looked perfect for the fedora-wearing, Tommy-toting gangster of the day. This one was the property of Oscar Varneau of Grand Rapids; he was a family man apparently doing pretty well. Out for a summer drive with his wife and son, he just pulled up at a roadside strawberry stand. Unfortunately for the Varneaus, the robbers pulled their soon-to-be-sputtering wheels up to the shoulder, grabbed their guns and money and claimed the car right before the family's stunned eyes.

That was also a short-term solution, it turns out. The Chrysler blew a tire along the stony back roads and they had to hijack yet another car, and this time they waved down a set of wheels ridden by four college kids.

WHEN THEY GOT TO THEIR HIDEOUT TO SPLIT UP THE TAKE, THEY WERE GLAD TO HEAR THAT NOBODY HAD DIED IN THE BANK MELEE. They didn't need that degree of heat on their heels. There had been some civilian injuries, though nothing life-threatening. And only one of the gang had been captured — Harry Harris, whose real name was Earl Doyle. He pleaded guilty and was sentenced to life in prison for the robbery.

In the days and weeks that followed, police from Grand Haven down to Benton Harbor combed the woods and dunes and knocked on doors just in case any of the thugs had stayed back or any other citizens had made their acquaintances. They came up empty-handed.

One other suspect was arrested in the aftermath, though. That was Ted Bentz, the half-brother of Eddie Bentz. He maintained his innocence all along, but was convicted and sent to Marquette State Prison.

Much later, police had an opportunity to ask Eddie if Ted had actually been part of the heist. He clammed up, so Ted's quest to clear his name marched onward. Ted spent much of his time in the pen writing letters to lawyers and judges, studying law and preparing legal briefs for fellow prisoners. He also wrote a regular outdoor column for the *Marquette Mining Journal* from his cell. Eventually, the mayor of Grand Haven saw the injustice and began to champion Ted's innocence. Perseverance eventually paid off and he won his freedom. The misunderstanding had only cost him 21 years of his life. Through it all, Ted's wife bravely spoke out that it was Ed, not Ted, who was in on the Grand Haven robbery.

Sometime after the Grand Haven debacle, Bentz returned to Brooklyn, New York, where he enjoyed his passions of collecting rare books and coins, and pulling off the occasional, well-planned heist. His last holdup was in Dansville, Vermont. On March 13, 1936, the Feds tracked him to his Brooklyn residence and found him hiding in a dumbwaiter. He was sentenced to 20 years and sent to the infamous prison on Alcatraz Island, off the coast of San Francisco. He was paroled in 1948 and died on October 31, 1979, of a heart attack at the age of 85.

OTHER MEMBERS OF THE ROBBING PARTY DID REMAIN IN MICHIGAN. Still, they were a transient lot, so the personnel tended to change from job to job. By 1936, Feds put out word that Bentz and at least nine other suspects — including Earl "Harry Harris" Doyle — were implicated in several different Michigan robberies, some of which occurred in the late 1920s. Shaken-down banks included:

- Sturgis National Bank for $80,000
- Lee State Bank of Dowagiac for $56,000
- Albion State Bank for $100,000
- People's Savings Bank of Cadillac for $162,000

While only four gunmen were involved in the Grand Haven robbery, the press released a list of suspects for that and other Michigan heists that included this list of associates:

- Tommy Carroll, killed in a fight with St. Paul, Minn., police.
- Homer Wilson, died of natural causes in 1934.
- Charles J. Fitzgerald, in federal prison accused of a kidnapping in St. Paul.
- "Campbell", first name unknown, killed by rival gangsters in Red Wing, Minn.
- James L. Ripley, accomplice in Bentz's Dansville, Vt., robbery.
- Edward Larue, a convict at United States Penitentiary in Leavenworth, Kan., for taking a stolen car across state lines. That became a federal crime in 1919, with the Dyer Act.
- Fred Goetz, killed in a Chicago gang war. He had been a member of the Fred Burke-Gus Winkler gang.
- Lee Turner, a St. Louis gangster and suspected participant in the Holland heist.

Believe Michigan Bank Robber Will Be Taken with Dillinger

When John Dillinger, Public Enemy No. 1, is captured, Lieutenant Van Loomis of the detective division of the Michigan state police believes the man pictured here will be taken with him.

He is Edward W. Bentz, alias E. R. Ronaldson, alias Ted Dewey. The picture shown here of him has been identified by a number of Michigan people as the photo of a man who had a part in bank robberies at Sturgis, St. Johns, Cadillac, Albion and Grand Haven.

EDWARD W. BENTZ

Michigan state police have definite information that Bentz was with John Dillinger in Chicago a few days ago and are hopeful that the net thrown around the man who escaped from Crown Point and its woman sheriff may also trap Bentz. Michigan will immediately seek to extradite him and are confident most of the unsolved bank robberies on the Michigan list will be cleaned up if he can be brought back here.

The troopers have been trailing Bentz for several months and have authorities in every state on the lookout for him.

The loot of bank jobs in Michigan with which police are linking Bentz totals $315,360.

Bentz was once arrested by a Michigan state trooper but that was back in 1924 and he waived extradition and was turned over to Illinois authorities for theft of a car.

Bentz' record is two pages long and started prior to 1912 with arrest in Chicago on a rioting charge. He was arrested in Washington state for jail breaking in 1911 and in 1912 sent to the state penitentiary at Walla Walla, Wash., for burglary.

His first Michigan arrest was in 1922 in Detroit for store robbery and he was sent to Jackson prison to serve 1½ to 5 years.

The arrest by the state trooper was in Van Buren county for theft of a car in Illinois. Trooper Martz was the officer. The record shows a sentence at the state prison at Waupun, Wis., for burglary and arrests in Texas for bank robbery.

PALACE GARDEN CAFE ANNOUNCES ORCHESTRA

Clare Wilson and his orchestra will open a limited engagement at the Palace Garden restaurant and night club, 430 North Washington avenue, Saturday night. The band will present a distinctive style of modern dance rhythm, it is promised.

In addition to the music there will be a floor show. The orchestra includes an exceptional array of voices including George Ramsley, Kenneth King, and George Newman, recently of the Michigan Radio network.

Lansing State Journal; April 6, 1934.

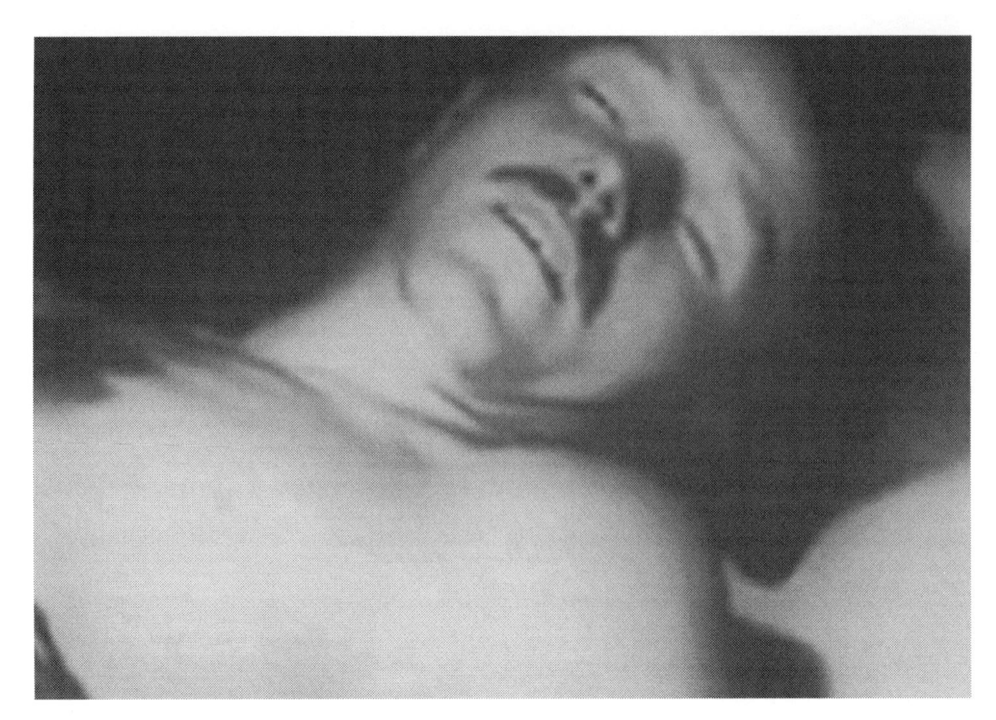

BAY FACE NELSON >>>>>>>>>>>>>>

In November, 1934, Nelson was shot nine times. A single machine gun slug struck his abdomen and eight shotgun pellets hit his legs. "I'm done for," he told his wife before giving his driver directions to a safe house in Wilmette. He died in bed with his wife at his side.

It's believed that once Baby Face got back to Chicago after the Grand Haven heist, he executed Freddie for leaving the group in the lurch. Then he went on to do the things that made his name. Back in August of '33, though, he was pretty much anonymous to the public. Only later did it become clear that the good citizens of Grand Haven had come face-to-face with one of the most volatile and violent of the Depression era's thugs.

Nelson hooked up with the Dillinger gang in early '34. He was with them at the Little Bohemia hideout in northern Wisconsin when the FBI staged its famous raid on the hoodlum holiday. Nelson shot three cops. One of them died. He took to the woods, trudged a couple miles through the snow in natty wing-tips and imposed himself on the home of a terrified Chippewa family. He stayed as an armed guest for three days.

His ultimate promotion to infamy came just a couple of months later when Feds shot Dillinger dead outside Chicago's Biograph Theater. Dillinger's death anointed Nelson the new Public Enemy No. 1. People who obtain that title don't tend to keep it for long, and Baby Face was no exception. On November 22, four months into his new title, he was in a car with his wife and another man heading south on U.S. 12, when he and a Fed in a northbound car locked eyes. They both skidded into a U-turn — the law and the outlaw looking for a fight. They both lost.

Jumping out of their cars, they blasted away at each other. One bullet tore through Nelson's gut. Time and blood ran out for him, but not before he sank the fatal slugs into federal officers Ed Hollis and Samuel Cowley.

Capone's cell at Philadelphia's Eastern State Penitentiary where he was imprisoned in May 1929.

OTHER FAMOUS FACES IN MICHIGAN >>>>>>>>

Several of the more famous criminals in American lore, primarily of the 1920s and '30s, have had dealings in Michigan, whether they were hiding out, meeting with cohorts, or simply taking a jaunt into the state to commit the rare crime here. Here are some sightings and legends of their dealings here.

AL CAPONE is synonymous with the decadence and violence of Chicago in the 1920s, but he often had good reason to skip town to a relatively low-key location after a high-profile hit. There are dozens of stories in the state about "Scarface" cooling his heels in Michigan.

One of his haunts was a club on stilts over Lake Lansing in Haslett, Michigan. Capone is said to have gone there to party. Conveniently, a trap door in the floor was always at the ready for the disposal of troublesome people, booze or damning evidence. While in the area, he often ate at Emil's Restaurant in Lansing. Capone is also said to have made an occasional foray up to his vacation home two miles south of Leland, across Lake Michigan and to the north from the stress of providing illegal hooch to the Chicagoans and other Midwesterners at a time when all hootch was illegal. The Prohibition-era vice king reputedly cooled his heels at a vacation home that was fitted with a lookout tower on a hill, while armed guards kept lookout at the gate. Constantine, Michigan, is another site where he's said to have had a "safe house," and where he may also have disposed of bodies. In an area nearby called Purgatory, graffitied ruins, foundations, and such are said to have been an underground bunker. The mob boss is just one of the many notables believed to have stayed at the House of Ludington in Escanaba. While Johnny Cash, John Phillip Sousa and Henry Ford could let it be known that they'd stayed there, Capone's lodging is unproven rumor, as are the presence of underground tunnels and stashes of Prohibition alcohol.

Bohm Theater, 1920s.

Capone got much of the illegal liquor he sold from Detroit's most infamous mob, the Purple Gang. A huge portion of what they imported from Canada was trucked west on Michigan Avenue to the Windy City. It was a huge operation, and from time to time the two gangs arranged for representatives to discuss the details. They needed a neutral place to meet. Legend has it that one of the regular places was the Bohm Theater in Albion. The representatives met in a row of four balcony seats right under the projection booth, away from the other moviegoers and close enough to the noise of the projector to allow them to negotiate and make plans without the rest of the audience noticing. There are now four seats in the balcony upholstered in purple as a reminder. The gang had many reputed hangouts in the state, including the Graceland Ball Room in Lupton, north of West Branch.

JOHN DILLINGER was said to have been in Sault Ste. Marie in April 1934, right after robbing a police station in Warsaw, Indiana, for weapons. He was hiding out as the house guest of fellow gang member John Hamilton's sister. When the Feds arrived on April 20, he was already gone. That same day he arrived at the Little Bohemia Lodge in the northern Wisconsin town of Manitowish Waters, where he and other gangsters would be involved in a well-known and bloody shootout with the law two days later.

BONNIE AND CLYDE, the glamour couple of Depression-era criminals, left a trail of robbery and murder in their native Texas, as well as Oklahoma, Arkansas, Missouri, and as far north as Iowa, MInnesota and Indiana before being shot to death in a police ambush in Louisiana. But mysteriously, two cars that they stole, both Fords, showed up in Jackson, giving investigators key bits of evidence in their man/woman hunt, including items found in the cars, like a medicine bottle prescribed to Clyde's aunt.

Bonnie Elizabeth Parker.

Clyde Barrow sent a letter to Henry Ford, extolling the virtue of his company's V-8 engines in running away from the cops. "While I still have got breath in my lungs I will tell you what a dandy car you make," he wrote, adding, "I have drove Fords exclusivly (sic) when I could get away with one."

Some question the letter's authenticity, and the criminal's praise never made it into celebrity-endorsement ads. It is now an artifact owned by the Henry Ford Museum of American Innovation in Dearborn.

ZOMBIE APOCALYPSE

THE YEAR: 2011 – 2015
THE CRIME: MULTIPLE BANK ROBBERIES
THE MOTIVE: PREPARING FOR ARMAGEDDON

STEVEN TIMOTHY SNYDER WAS RIPPED. THE PHOTOS THAT CIRCULATED WHEN HE BECAME OF PUBLIC INTEREST SHOW A GUY WHO FILLS OUT A SWEATER LIKE A MARVEL COMIC CHARACTER. A ROCK-LIKE CHEST AND DON'T-MESS-WITH-ME 'CEPS. He worked out to maintain it, and he chopped, kicked and grappled his way through mixed martial arts competitions.

But it wasn't for the sake of vanity and he didn't sweat it out for health. It was for the ultimate fight; the final fight for survival. He was going to be left standing when the government and society collapsed, a development he figured was imminent. When it happened, he'd be ready to defend himself however necessary.

Snyder wasn't new to adopting extreme views. Twenty years earlier, he'd run with a skinhead, white-supremacist group in Wisconsin, known as the Fond du Lac Boot Boys. Nowadays, he was determined to be ready with stockpiled food, water and munitions for the ultimate end-game. The G's he grabbed hold of in bank jobs helped.

Snyder's career spanned nine bank holdups over four years. He was knocking down mostly small town banks and generally crossed the state to do his crimes. At least in the beginning, he targeted towns small enough to not have their own police forces. From a small town himself, he was among the 500 people who called Kingston, in the middle of the Thumb, home.

That's not to say he was a nickel-and-dime bandit. He had at least one six-figure payday among those one-horse-town robberies. Courtesy was part of his currency— he was known as the "Respectful Robber" because he reputedly held a door for a woman during one caper. Also, he didn't swear while he threatened people for money.

It all started on June 3, 2011, with the inauspicious-looking Lake Osceola State Bank in the tiny commercial strip of Luther. He hit another Lake Osceola branch later that month, this time in Wellston, between Cadillac and Manistee.

He didn't strike again until that December, but this one was a biggie and people started to take notice. The victim institution this time was the Citizens National Bank in Pellston, which is near the tip of the Lower Peninsula and goes by the nickname "Icebox of the Nation" because it's one of those handful of places that frequently hits the weather reports for its overnight lows bottoming out the entire U.S.A.

Citizens National put the word out that a tall, slender, white man strode inside with a semi-automatic handgun. He wore a puffy, blue coat, mirrored aviator sunglasses, a fur bomber hat and a camouflage bandanna over his face. By the time he took off in a tan sedan, he had $100,000 in cold cash from the Icebox. Of course, the getaway car was stolen, and he abandoned it a few miles east of the robbery to switch to another ride that hadn't been eyeballed by the witnesses to the crime.

Then, he seems to have taken a break, for almost two years. A hit in Croton Township, west of Newaygo, was the last Michigan bank he knocked down. From now on, he would travel out of state for his holdups.

Snyder escaped attention for the robberies themselves for a long time, though his unusual behavior at home raised some eyebrows for different reasons. For one thing, he was spending a lot of time and sweat digging a tunnel under his house. He filled the tunnel with canned food and other non-perishables and water for the dystopian chaos he was expecting.

UP TO THIS POINT, IT WAS SAID THAT THE WELL-MANNERED CRIMINAL HAD NOT HURT ANYBODY DURING HIS ROBBERIES. Unfortunately, his wife, Stacey, was not receiving the benefit of that courtesy. When he wasn't preaching to her about the coming "Zombie Apocalypse", he bossed her and smacked her around. On Christmas day, 2014, she'd taken the last abuse she was going to take and called the police. Now, there was a domestic violence warrant out for his arrest.

Then, in March, while living apart from him, Stacey saw a news story about a robbery. When they played the tape from the security camera, she recognized him. She'd actually known of his extra-curricular activities since 2011, when she noticed him poring over newspaper articles about robberies that always seemed to happen right around the time he'd shave his goatee. "Is that you?" she asked, pointing to the news item that was obviously fascinating him. He copped to Luther and Wellston. "But if you tell the cops," he warned, "you'll never see the kids again."

Now three years later, the Christmas assault separated them. As the crust of winter wore on and began to wear out, she began to feel a slightly safer distance from him. So with him showing up on grainy surveillance vids gone viral, and the kids at a hopefully safe distance, Stacey told police what she knew. Police detectives in Michigan, Ohio and Wisconsin plus federal agents, started teleconferencing, calling, sharing clues and narratives to see if it was the same guy and to figure out what he might do next.

St Louis Post Dispatch; Mar 26, 2015.

ASSOCIATED PRESS

Officers work the scene Tuesday where a Wisconsin State Patrol trooper just three months out of the academy died in a shootout with a bank robbery suspect. The robbery suspect was also killed in the shootout.

Snyder's long crime spree culminated on the morning of March 25. He started the day 60 miles north of Green Bay, in Wausaukee, Wisconsin. He figured he'd drop off his car outside of town, then walk to the bank, kind of like he'd done in Pellston. He could steal a bank employee's car, then drive to his parked car and take off. Hopefully, that would put the cops onto the scent of the employee's car and buy a few minutes or more in the getaway.

Yet when he stopped to park his car, he chose a spot that happened to be Thomas Christ's property. Christ came driving up in his truck just as Snyder was parking and told him to move it. Snyder shot Christ and then headed for the bank.

He pulled off the job at the State Bank of Florence in Wausaukee and robbed a teller's car in the process. This time, he wasn't about to go back to the car he'd parked. There was now a dead body there. So he drove south on Highway 141, observing the speed limit, for about two hours. When he got to Fond du Lac, a Wisconsin State patrolman recognized the car from police bulletins.

Mourners wait in line Sunday for Wisconsin State Trooper Trevor Casper's funeral in Kiel.

GARY C. KLEIN/GANNETT WISCONSIN MEDIA

The Post Crescent; Mar 30, 2015.

Wisconsin Trooper Trevor Casper, a rookie who was working his first solo shift ever, had the sour luck of spotting the three-state fugitive just hours into what should have been speeding tickets and ambulance assists. He began following the car from a distance. No sirens, no flashers. Yep, this is the one in the Wausaukee thing, and now there's a body up there, too.

Snyder had been keeping a keen eye on that rear-view for 120 miles now. Any hint of a shield on a door or a searchlight by the side-view mirror captured his immediate attention. This state car lagging back was a problem, and he knew it. The cop had to be talking on the radio, and his friends would appear from the side streets any minute now.

Then, right by the Pick N Save, Snyder yanked his wheel into a sharp turn to face the suspicious cop. He left the car in drive, jumped out and fired on the trooper. Casper leaped out of the state car just like the crook, right down to leaving the car in gear. As the driverless machines drifted awkwardly toward curbs and parking lots, the two men bolted around and traded shots in a rapid volley of gunfire. Twenty-one shots; nine from the robber, 12 from the cop. Casper went down as Snyder staggered toward a condo development.

Flashing blue and white lights grew larger and closer and filled the morning with their hellishly dazzling dance in front of the condos. Bullet-vested SWAT-types inched toward the grounds and found Snyder lying lifeless on the brown grass. A single slug from Casper's Glock pierced his chest.

Back closer to the discount mart, the freshly-anointed cop lay victim of three slugs from Snyder: neck, chest and left hand. At 21, Casper was the youngest trooper to ever die in the line of duty for America's Dairyland.

HOW MANY ROBBERIES END IN FATALITIES? >>>>>>>>

In 2016, there were 4,251 robberies of banks and other financial institutions in the United States, with eight resulting deaths. Seven of the people killed were the perpetrators and one was an employee, according to FBI statistics.
Ten years prior, in 2006, there were 7,272 such robberies, with 13 deaths, including 10 perpetrators, one employee, one cop and one guard.

The number of robberies in Michigan in those years: 101 in '16 and 246 in '06. The FBI Bank Crime Statistics report does not indicate in which states the fatalities occurred.

DEATH BY GUN >>>>>>>>

The Centers for Disease Control reports that 38,658 people were killed by guns in the United States in 2016. That's 12 people out of every 100,000, up from 11 of 100,000 a year earlier.

About two-thirds of gun deaths are suicides.

ONE DAY JUSTICE

THE YEAR: 1930
THE CRIME: A FIRST CRACK AT LAWLESSNESS
THE MOTIVE: NO HONEST WORK TO BE FOUND

THE AIR WAS AS CRISP AS A CORN FLAKE WHEN JAMES GALLAGHER AND THOMAS MARTIN PULLED UP IN FRONT OF THE OLD MERCHANTS BANK & TRUST CO. IN DOWNTOWN BATTLE CREEK. THE BANK WAS IN THE BASE OF THE 18-STORY BUILDING ON WEST MICHIGAN THAT BORE ITS NAME.

Gallagher had lived in Battle Creek a few months earlier, working for the Oliver tractor factory. Several times, he'd gone to the Old Merchants bank to cash checks and, while standing in line, he'd looked over the lay of the lobby, the teller windows and the vaults and fantasized about a robbery. Gallagher would have been a newcomer to the criminal business had he acted then. He didn't, yet his bored musings in the teller line didn't vanish when he heard "next" from one of the windows.

Thomas Martin, an acquaintance of Gallagher's from Gary, Indiana, also had a clean criminal slate. Both lived most of the time in Gary, and that's where Gallagher returned after getting laid off from the Oliver factory. It was pretty much the infancy of the Great Depression, so their prospects for finding honest work were as grim as the next guy's. And it was starting to feel like just about everybody was the next guy.

Whether out of frustration with grumbling stomachs and worn out clothes, or just for something to talk about, Gallagher told Martin about his observations at the bank in Battle Creek. Martin was intrigued with the idea of the easy score — he could also use a quick payday. Within a week, they figured they'd give it a whirl. In the two-day lead-up, they whetted their appetites on auto theft, swiping a Ford in Gary. They drove it to Fort Wayne, where they found a Hudson sedan ripe for the picking. That would become their wheels to and from the bank in Cereal City.

When they got to town, they rented a room for the night at the Faust Hotel, signing in as James Burgess and Thomas Summers of South Bend. They anxiously killed time that evening, going over

the escape route they were sure would get them quickly out of town and back home. In the morning, they grabbed a pillowcase from the hotel as a loot sack, then waited through the lunch-hour rush — watching, waiting and working up the nerve to pull it off. They did work it up, too. They hadn't come this far for a vacation.

AS MOST OF BATTLE CREEK RETURNED TO WORK FOR THE AFTERNOON, Martin took a position at the bank entrance while Gallagher sauntered up to a free teller cage. He said he'd like to open an account. Barely looking up, the bank manager slipped him a form and asked him to fill it out. When he glanced up again, he saw the customer was pointing something at him, and it wasn't a pen.

At that moment, a 25-year-old woman customer came up in line, too close for the young thug's comfort. He pushed her to the next window. She was about to complain about the rude man, then realized that he was no customer at all. "Look straight ahead!" he snapped. "Act like nothing's happening." She gulped and did as she was told while the teller scooped $2,260 (a $32,000 haul now) in paper and coin into the bandit's pillowcase.

Meanwhile, the novice crooks decided to herd the two employees and two women doing their banking into the vault to keep them that much farther from sounding the alarm. At least, Martin and Gallagher hoped it would buy them a few steps out the door, maybe even a good stomp on the gas pedal before hell got unleashed.

As the drama inside the bank unfolded, Herbert Buroker was parked at the curb in front with his baby on the seat next to him. He happened to look through the bank window just as some guy shoved his wife. He was about ready to barge in and give that rude sonofagun a piece of his mind when he realized there was something more going on. He waited in his car and saw the two thieves rush out. He watched as the pillowcase ripped open, spilling the money by the doorway. The crooks cursed the useless hotel linen and tossed it aside, frantically grabbing handfuls of cash and stuffing it in their coat pockets.

The men hopped into the heisted Hudson, which happened to be parked right in front of Buroker's car. As they fired up the engine and sped away, Buroker urged C.F. Radtke, who was standing by the curb, to get in the car with him, presumably to hold the baby while Buroker put his Essex coupe in gear and got right on the crooks' tail. Gallagher and Martin had to ditch the getaway route they'd hoped to take, and now needed to improvise on streets they didn't know. They'd found the streets of least resistance, but couldn't shake the self-deputized nuisance behind them. Buroker stayed in their rear view mirror, matching them turn for turn, forcing them into a maze of strange roads. They were getting hopelessly lost and kept trying to take the southward and westward routes that should get them to familiar territory.

Buroker kept up with them for miles, at times pulling up next to the getaway car, trying to bump it off the side of the road while Radtke braced himself against the sharp turns, playing car-seat to his baby. There were no seat belts, let alone car seats.

As Buroker's gas gauge teetered on empty somewhere around Beadle Lake, some four miles south of town, he resigned himself to giving up the chase. He parked, ran into a drug store and called the police with a license number and description of the car and the men in it. Police welcomed the clues. They added it to some the pair had left behind, like the pillowcase with the name of the hotel embroidered in it. The top brass were assigning dicks to talk to the hotel clerks, and others to interview the victims in the bank. Still others coordinated with cop stations to the south. Dispatchers broadcast the plate number, descriptions of the thugs, late sightings and the like on the state-of-the-art, one-way police radio system.

The robbers hoped to outrun the mounting army against them and blast through before barricades could go up. A mile north of Burr Oak, Trooper John S. Burke was sent by his commanding officer at White Pigeon post to look for the suspects on motorcycle. He caught sight of the car and chased after them. When he motioned them to the shoulder, they slowed to a stop on the gravel and grass. Trooper Burke got off his bike and walked toward the car. When he got to their window, Martin panicked, shot him through the neck and they sped away. The body would be found about 4 p.m., so in less than two hours, Martin and Gallagher had become two of the most serious kinds of felon, armed robbers and murderers.

Troopers Edd Freeman and Dan Wurzburg wanted to find the sonsofbitches, now that they were cop killers. They went south of Coldwater and over the state line, playing some hunches. When they stopped to ask a farmer if he'd seen the suspect car, he pointed in the direction they were already headed. Before long, the officers saw the car stopped at the side of the road, abandoned. Its gas tank and radiator were both bone dry from the hard ride and smoked an acrid, metallic odor into the air.

The officers noticed some footprints and slowly drove forward, following the sandy tracks for two miles. When they came within sight of the two men walking on the side of the road, the bandits looked back. Seeing the police car, they both bolted for opposite sides of the road.

The troopers hopped out of the car and split up: Freeman went after Martin, who fumbled in his pocket for a pistol as he ran. As Martin's hand came out with the gun, Freeman stopped to steady his shot and pinged the weapon right out of Martin's hand.

Wurzburg only had to shoot the ground next to Gallagher before he gave up.

The officers drove the cop killers back to Sturgis and locked them in heavily guarded jail cells. Even the outside of the jail was surrounded by armed lawmen, in case anyone might come and try to spring the two. Upward of 300 people stopped what they were doing to stand vigil outside the building, hoping for a glimpse of the criminals who had dominated news and gossip all day.

In the middle of the night, police drove the two suspects to the courthouse in Centreville, where they readily spilled their guts to a state lieutenant and a prosecutor. They confessed to both the robbery and the murder. In an emergency session the next morning, Judge Glenn E. Warner sentenced them to life in prison, and before the morning was over they were shackled and transported to what would be their new permanent residence: the maximum security state prison in Jackson. So by the time of the 24-hour anniversary of turning to crime, they were each living in a one-room efficiency apartment behind steel bars and eating off metal trays.

In the aftermath, with the public and press lauding the quick dispensation of justice, police recommended that Buroker receive a reward for his brave — albeit foolish — chasing of the bandits. Buroker was honored for providing the police with invaluable information. They also believed that his dogged pursuit on the first leg of their escape flight rattled the inexperienced duo into making costly mistakes.

No word on how that baby felt, thereafter, about getting in the car with dad.

HIGH-SPEED PURSUITS OF LAW BREAKERS

>>>>>>>

Police chases are a staple of YouTube. Yet while they can be exciting to watch, it's a dangerous pursuit that often ends in disaster, and one of the most dangerous parts of police work.

- In 2012, the most recent year recorded, there were an estimated 68,000 police car chases in the United States, according to the Department of Justice.
- For the last 20 years, an estimated 355 people per year are killed as a result of chases. That includes passengers, pedestrians and police.
- An estimated 2 percent of local police departments prohibit high-speed pursuits.
- Michigan had 300 pursuit-related fatalities from 1996 to 2015.

THE SILENT VISITOR

THE YEAR: 1978
THE CRIME: SNEAKING INTO HOMES
THE MOTIVE: SCARING AND ROBBING

MARVIN WATSON WAS A QUIET MAN. TOO QUIET.

For instance, he would show up in someone's house, standing over them while they were just waking up or watching TV. All of a sudden, a chilling hunch, a glance and there's a 36-year-old guy with a mask over his face standing in the middle of your house or over your bed, first thing in the morning.

Marvin started this stunt for the first time we know of on May 6, 1978, at a Battle Creek home in what's known as the Post Addition (see next page). By the time the homeowner noticed him, he'd been inside for God-knows-how-long. In this and other burglaries, he'd open the basement window, climb inside and patiently listen to the life upstairs, waiting for it to settle somewhere. Then he'd inch, catlike, toward the stairs.

Marvin Watson — an unemployed, former administrator of a community-service group — terrified his senior victims beyond the initial jolt of seeing a stranger in one's own home, safe zone, fortress. He hit some of them, and taped and tied them, then looted the home for cash, jewelry and valuables.

His escapades moved on out of the Addition and found victims in more rural areas after his first few break-ins. Then he hit Kalamazoo, Albion and Lansing.

He became known as the "Basement Bandit," with a string of 11 burglaries. When a crook gets a nickname, you know they're going to be a high priority for the police. And it was in Lansing, more than a year after he'd started, when police caught him on the roof of a house. He jumped down and shattered his ankle. He just couldn't hop away fast enough and police grabbed him … to the collective relief of seniors in south-central Michigan.

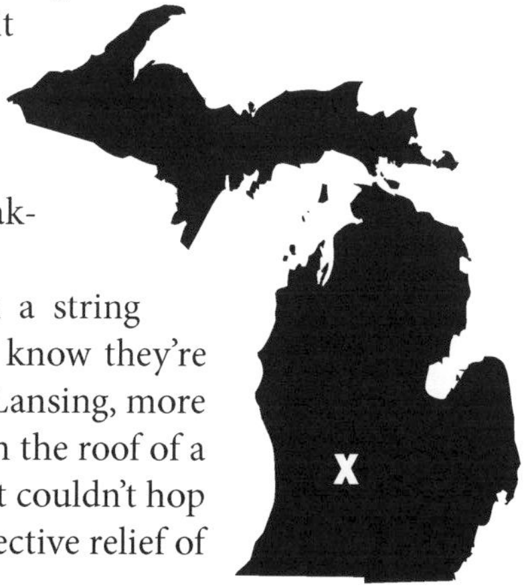

Breathing exercises at the Battle Creek Sanitarium.

THE POST ADDITION >>>>>>>>>>>>

If you're in Battle Creek and hear about the Post Addition, it doesn't have anything to do with sugar or raisins and it's not a good source of Omega-3s. The Post Addition is a sizable neighborhood on the east side of the city, overlooked by a factory with the red oval Post logo, just like on a box of raisin bran, congenial as a red notice at the top of Facebook. And the neighborhood was designed by none other than C.W. Post, the second-most famous Battle Creek cereal magnate.

Originally from Springfield, Illinois, Charles William Post had been in several lines of business and had always done well. But each enterprise would eventually end with him a frazzle of nerves. He quit a gig manufacturing farm machinery in Kansas and as a real-estate developer in Texas, leaving when the stress got to be too much. He traveled the globe by ship and train in search of a cure for his fragile nerves, eventually checking himself into John Harvey Kellogg's renowned Battle Creek Sanitarium in 1891. Kellogg was running the trendy health emporium on the edge of town in a building that would expand to a 14-story tower ... until the Depression, when hunger pangs took the place of trend diets.

Post was impressed with Kellogg and his health and well-being regimens, particularly the odd-but-delicious practice of eating flaked and baked grains submerged in milk. The student soon became a competitor of his teacher's brother.

First, though, Post opened a plant to make his new company's first grain-based product. It was the beverage called Postum, a powder to be mixed with warm water as a substitute to coffee. The company then branched out to Grape-Nuts, those crunchy breakfast pebbles that have nothing to do with grapes or nuts. Eventually, Post's company expanded into corn flakes. He first named them Elijah's Manna. That name may have been perfectly fitting with the florid, curlicued, Victorian world of the 19th Century, but at that time, Post, Battle Creek and everyone else roared into the 20th, which would be dominated by simple, non-religion-

based, corporate names and logos. So before long, the product was re-christened as Post Toasties. Incidentally, Kellogg's first company name was also devoid of any snap, crackle or pop. It was the Battle Creek Toasted Corn Flake Company. But that got shortened within a couple of successful decades to just the family name, apostrophe S. In those days, both Post and Kellogg were making the breakfast-cereal habit a national health craze so that by mid-century, starting the day with milk on flakes seemed like the most natural thing in the world.

In the first couple of decades, as the dueling cereal factories hummed and grew, C.W. Post bought up land on the east side of town for the Post Addition, offering affordable housing for Post's employees. It was partly to keep them happy so they wouldn't unionize. And it provided good homes with a loan from the company that plant workers could pay off with minimal pain. Business boomed in the bullish '20s, and there were always new houses going up in the Addition. Families moved in and spent the next half century living in a thriving sub-habitat of the Creek, with neighborhood shops a short walk away.

As the Post and Kellogg workforces were whittled down to a fraction of their former selves, the city and the Addition have suffered. A once working-class haven, the Addition has become known for high unemployment, blight and crime.

Back to C.W. Post's story: In 1910, his company was fined $50,000 in response to a lawsuit that questioned a claim that Grape-Nuts cured appendicitis, an illness that afflicted Post himself. In 1914, he put a gun to his head and killed himself, partly, it's believed, because of his relentless stomach pain. His daughter, Marjorie Merriweather Post, inherited the business and saw it through decades of continued growth.

DISAPPEARANCE OF A BASTARD

THE YEAR: 1870s
THE CRIME: PIMPING AND ASSAULT
THE MOTIVE: ENSLAVING WOMEN FOR PROFIT

THE IRON SMELTERS IN FAYETTE, AT THE TIP OF GARDEN PENINSULA, BURNED BRIGHT FROM 1867 TO 1891. For 24 years Fayette's working people made pig iron from rusty rocks gouged out of dank, lightless holes in the red roads of the northwestern U.P. Iron ore was shipped the short distance from Escanaba to Fayette to be made into pig iron, which was then shipped on to steel mill towns on the Great Lakes and beyond.

When the smelting company declared Fayette a dry town in the 1870s, an enterprising old miser, Alphonse Berlanquette, started the Hole in the Ground saloon, just outside the bustling and largely isolated settlement. His bar was on the shore of Sand Bay and received regular shipments of liquor from Green Bay. But he died while Fayette was still happening — and gave rise to a hidden treasure legend (see page 44). That left an opening for Jim Summers to serve the ready-made clientele. But Summers took it further. Men in town or on the lake had more than one kind of thirst, so he figured he'd sell female companionship by the hour or the deed, whichever was quicker.

Summers got women the way many pimps did — kidnap, trickery, indentured servitude or by the woman's choice. He had a cruel reputation, but it was a line of work largely built on cruelty. He beat his sex slaves and people in the area knew it. He was widely despised, though it's unlikely that distaste for his personality damaged his commerce. His undoing came when the townspeople got to know a young woman tricked into his employ.

Summers had placed an ad in a Milwaukee newspaper, seeking a female caretaker and companion for his ailing wife. He found someone young and eager. She answered the posting, packed her bags and lugged them onto the next Goodrich line steamer bound for the remote, yet booming Upper Peninsula.

X

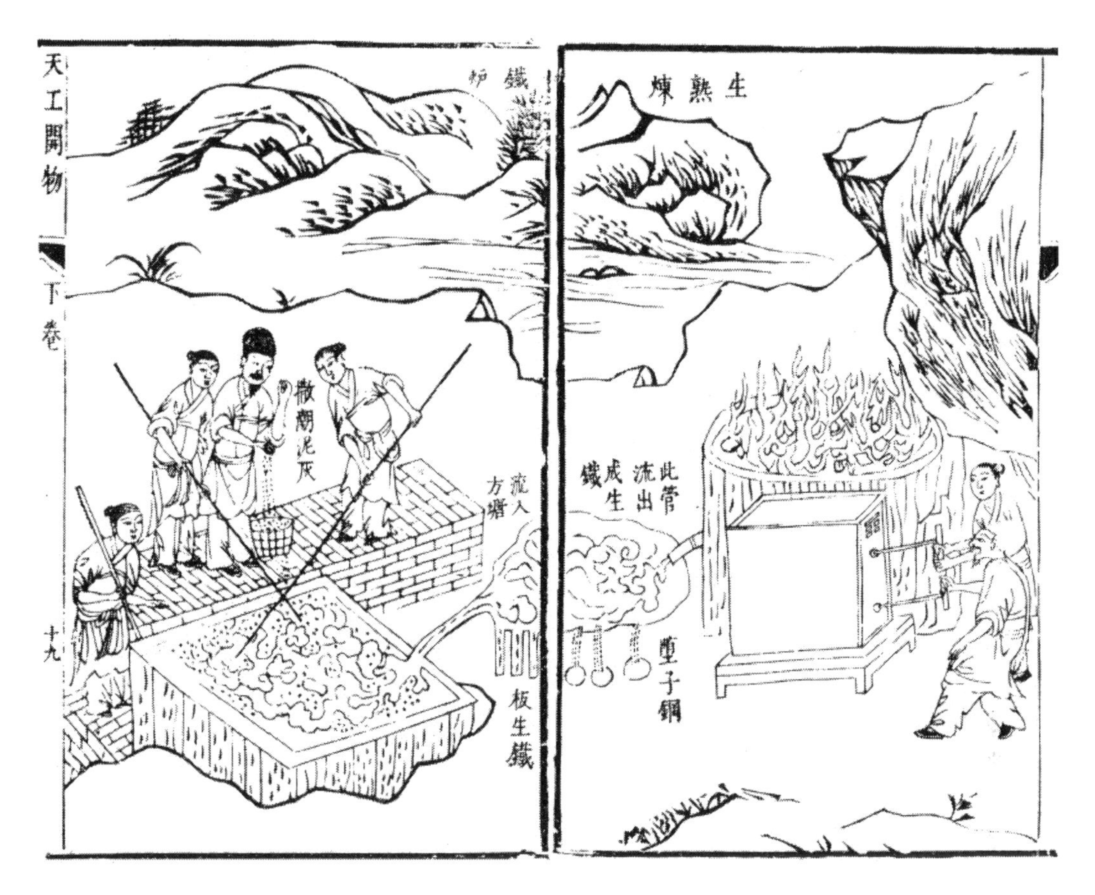

These drawings from the Tiangong Kaiwu encyclopedia, printed in 1637, illustrate iron smelting. On the left, men are engaged in the fining process, making wrought iron from pig iron. On the right, men work a blast furnace to produce pig iron.

We don't know her name, but she ingratiated herself to those at J.A. Harris's hotel in Fayette as a friendly and likable young woman; not at all the kind of harlot that might go to work at Summers' place. It's likely she mentioned or showed someone the misleading ad. Whether out of fear of the volatile Summers, or for not wanting to get involved, they apparently let her go to his house. When she got there, she saw no one who looked like a sickly, older woman. She saw the sleazy Summers, his sidekick known as Fatty and three or four women not far from her own age. She realized what she was getting into, and when she objected, he beat her savagely. She ran back toward the loud, bustling, iron-smelting burg where her steamliner ride had landed. Summers, who obviously wanted her as property, followed, determined to drag her back, literally, if necessary.

But this clever girl knew the town was where he'd look first. And, after all, the nice people of Fayette had let her walk into the den of the beast. Unsure who they'd back in a showdown, she got around a bend and cut sharply into the woods. She let things cool for a couple of days, eating wild berries. The company of wild animals might be territorial, but it was never malicious.

At last, she flagged down a logging train, and the conductor brought her back to town and to a hotel. When Summers sneaked in and kidnapped her, it was torch and pitchfork time, said Hugh Stephens, who lived through it and recounted it some 60 years later. Participants also recounted that 500 or so men and boys, feeding on each other's angry energy, set out for Summers' property to beat him to a pulp. No word on how many of the hasty volunteer army had already seen the upstairs boudoirs of the Summers ranch under different circumstances.

Before they got where they were going, someone spread the news that the rat Summers was at "Pig Iron Fred" Hink's tavern, taking out his violent temper on the proprietors and their stock and furnishings. The angry mob detoured, found him in mid-rampage and dragged him out of the bar. With everyone wanting to get his licks in, Summers was soon knocked to the ground. Men and boys continued to unleash kicks and stomps on what had become a limp, unresponsive bag of meat and leaking blood.

When body-kicking got old, they turned toward Summers' house, swarming in to ransack the place for money. Two thousand dollars was found in Fatty's room, which they all agreed should go to the unfortunate women in Summers' employment. That meant boat fare home for the young lady who blew the whistle on the creep and starter cash for the others.

Now, some of the righteous throng figured it was time to bury the whoremaster Summers' corpse before it became as fetid as his soul. But when they got to the spot where they last saw him lying broken and bloody, there was no body. Could it be that the rotten cuss survived the pulverizing they'd just dealt him? Still, he couldn't have walked away in his condition. Could he? No sign visible by lantern or torch of wolves dragging him away for a feast, either. It appeared that Fatty and friends must have quickly carted him away to bury him or nurse him back to health.

Townsfolk debated Summers' fate for years to come. Rumors had him showing up in a bar fight here, or there. According to some, he even reopened a brothel in Iron Mountain.

Above: "Brothel" by Joachim Beuckelaer, 1562.

Below: U.S. servicemen line up at the Recreation and Amusement Association during the Occupation of Japan.

BROTHELS IN 1913

>>>>>>>>

In 1913, women made up 44.6 million of the 92.2 million population of the United States, and the Justice Department figured that 100,000 of them were working as prostitutes in brothels. That was the result of a two-year study to determine the extent of the "white slavery" problem in America. Some, however, estimated the number to be as high as half a million.

Regardless, prostitution played a dark and sizable role in American history. Well, world history, for that matter. Behind the ruffly-dressed and painted women of old Western movies are far sadder tales of desperate women providing "comfort" to Western settlers, miners and gold-rushers, lumberjacks, and just about every place where men tended to outnumber women.

While the 1913 study shed some light on the extent of the world's oldest profession in this country, concern and activism to protect sex workers is still in its infancy. The problems facing prostitutes — disease, violence, drug addiction, exploitation — are as old as the practice itself.

MINERS' PAYROLL

THE YEAR: 1893
THE CRIME: TRAIN ROBBERY
THE MOTIVE: UNEMPLOYED WITH INSIDER KNOWLEDGE

A NARROW-GAUGE TRACK OF THE DULUTH, SOUTH SHORE & ATLANTIC RAILWAY RAN CARGO, PEOPLE AND MONEY BETWEEN CALUMET AND HOUGHTON, ABOUT 20 MILES, serving the many copper mines of Keweenaw Peninsula.

On a late-summer morning, as the train carried the monthly pay for legions of miners, four men, hiding behind masks, barged onto the train at a stop, about halfway between Calumet and Houghton. Two of the bandits held guns on the engineer and fireman while the others told the express messenger to load up a sack with as much of the payroll cash sent from the mining company bosses out East as they could.

They got a healthy $70,000 of that money, worth about the same as $1.9 million today, while a couple of the thugs went trick-or-treating for watches, jewelry and traveling cash from the passengers. The robbers slipped out at the next stop and sped away in a waiting horse and buggy.

Police figured whoever pulled the job off had some knowledge of that train, its schedule, and especially its cargo. They obviously knew that once every month, right in the middle, the train carried cash for Calumet & Hecla Mining Co. to pay its 2,000 or so workers.

The investigation led them first to George Kliberty, who did indeed know the train's schedule and cargo. He had recently been laid off from the rail line due to cost-cutting staff cuts. He had been employed as a fireman — not someone who puts out fires, but the guy who stokes the fire running the steam engine. With the help of witnesses and former co-workers, police came up with Kliberty as a suspect within two days. They obtained a warrant for his arrest and found him at his home.

Calumet & Hecla Mine shaft No. 2, about 1906.

Detectives chained him to an officer and loaded him onto a train bound for Houghton. Before they got there, he confessed to the whole thing and rolled over on the whole crew. Yep, they were also laid-off train workers. Seven suspects in all faced charges, including those who helped the four stickup guys escape after they got off the train with the money.

Finding the money, however, turned out to be more difficult. Yet they found a good chunk of it with the help of the Pinkertons, including William Pinkerton, son of the founder of the famous detective agency, as well as agents provided by a young company known as American Express.

Allan Pinkerton (on left) with Abraham Lincoln and Major General John A. McClernand.

Pinkerton was head of the Union Intelligence Service during the first two years of the Civil War. He sent agents undercover to pose as Confederate soldiers, providing military intelligence to the Union.

Pinkerton guards escort strikebreakers in Buchtel, Ohio, 1884.

PINKERTON DETECTIVES >>>>>>>>

Allan Pinkerton, who came to the U.S. from Glasgow, Scotland, started the Pinkerton National Detective Agency in 1850 in Chicago. A decade later, the Pinkertons made a name for themselves by thwarting an assassination attempt on President Abraham Lincoln, and then serving as his bodyguards. (Incidentally, it wasn't the Pinkertons that were shirking their duties when John Wilkes Booth succeeded in assassinating Honest Abe. That infamy belongs to John Parker, a Washington city cop, who left his post outside the President's balcony box at Ford's Theatre to find a seat where he could see the play, and later left to visit a saloon next door. (It's not clear where of the two places he was when Booth barged in and shot Lincoln, but then, it really doesn't matter, does it?)

During the Civil War, the agency performed military intelligence for the Union Army, in part by infiltrating Confederate groups. Later that century, banks and railroad companies hired them to go after Jesse James. At the same time, steel mills, lumbering companies and other big businesses contracted Pinkertons to bust unions and break strikes and identify rabble rousers and weed out union sympathizers.

Their reputation took a hit when, in 1892, they were hired to quell a strike in Homestead, Pennsylvania, and the clash turned bloody. Of the 16 people killed in the conflict, seven were Pinkerton agents. That's just part of why unions view the Pinkertons as adversaries.

In the 20th and 21st centuries, the Pinkertons were called on less and less as public police departments beefed up their own detective divisions. Lately, they've entered into security consultation, and in 2014, Pinkerton Consulting & Investigations Inc. moved its headquarters from New Jersey to Ann Arbor.

Pinkerton agents were hired to track outlaws like the Reno Gang, the James Gang and the Doolin–Dalton Gang.

Top: A photo of the Doolin-Dalton Gang, (aka The Wild Bunch). Front row, left to right: Harry A. Longabaugh (aka Sundance Kid), Ben Kilpatrick (aka Tall Texan), Robert Leroy Parker (aka Butch Cassidy). Standing: Will Carver and Harvey Logan (aka Kid Curry). Fort Worth, Texas, 1900.

Right: Harry Longabaugh (Sundance Kid) and Etta Place pose for a photo just before sailing to South America.

SHOOTOUT IN A BLIZZARD

THE YEAR: 1996
THE CRIME: BANK ROBBERY/HOSTAGE TAKING
THE MOTIVE: INNER DEMONS

IT WASN'T WELL PLANNED, BUT THEN THE MOTIVE REALLY WASN'T MONEY.

John Segreto boldly held up a bank on Sheldon Avenue close to the police department. In fact, the bank was on the same block! Police could likely run there faster than drive. And funny thing, Segreto had no car. He had to steal one from a bank employee during the robbery. He had bad timing too — the beginning of a blizzard was not ideal for a getaway chase.

But at 25, John Segreto was struggling with schizophrenia. He'd grown up in California and had been well-mannered and easy-going. Something changed, though, after he enrolled at Michigan Technological University. He overdid it with partying, dropped out and moved home. A couple years later, he went back to Tech, and this time, his behavior turned bizarre. He would disappear, and once even ended up in Switzerland, telling authorities that the U.S. government was trying to kill him.

He did the same thing in Vancouver, Canada, and was hospitalized there on a mental illness ward. He went back to southern California, but eventually made his way back to Houghton.

So there were apparently some serious interior demons tormenting Segreto when he took his .20-gage shotgun into the bank that afternoon. He demanded money, as bank robbers are wont to do. Segreto also wanted the keys to an employee's car, and a female hostage. Specifically a married woman.

Despite the slippery roads, slowing down the other cars inching through downtown Houghton, he made it out of town.

He took Tracy Immonen to a remote area and parked.

Police tracked him down and, hoping for a peaceful end to the crime, they brought along a psychologist to help with the negotiations. They'd hoped to help Immonen escape and get Segreto the help he needed.

But to complicate things, he'd strapped a homemade bomb to her.

Houghton County Sheriff's Deputy Sid Collins talks Thursday with John Segreto, who held a bank teller hostage in his car for hours after robbing the bank. Segreto was later shot and killed by police.

KEN STUROS/Daily Mining Gazette via Associated Press

Detroit Free Press; Jan 20, 1996.

Then, while police watched and hoped for a peaceful resolution, Segreto took out a kitchen knife, grabbed the ends of her brown hair and sliced off a handful. He waved it at the cops and tossed it out the window. In between hollering demands — he wanted to talk to President Clinton — he continued whacking away at her hair. It was a long, tense night, with heavy snowfall making things worse.

Around 6 in the morning, Segreto stepped it up a notch. "Next, it'll be her fingers," he yelled.

Police decided they couldn't wait any longer. The steadily falling flakes made it nearly impossible for even an experienced police marksman to pick the right shot. Yet the four state police sharpshooters fired four bullets through the car window and into Segreto's head, ending Tracy Immonen's night of terror and John Segreto's once-promising life, turned tragic at the hands of mental illness.

ROBBING THE DRUNKS

OR THERE'S NOTHING IN A NAME

THE YEAR: 1880s
THE CRIME: SEX-TRAFFICKING, MURDER, AND MANY MORE
THE MOTIVE: GREED

WE THINK OF MOST ROBBERS AS ROBBING UP. THEY ROB BANKS, TRAINS, THOSE WHO ARE WEALTHIER AND MORE POWERFUL THAN THEMSELVES IN ORDER TO GET SOME OF THAT SWEET SCRATCH. James Carr and Maggie Duncan, on the other hand, robbed down. They owned a successful brothel, yet they robbed, cheated and intimidated the rank-and-file lumber workers for their meager pay. And they tricked, drugged and kidnapped women into pleasing the working stiffs for the financial benefit of Jim and Maggie.

Harrison is a burg of 2,100 people around the lush, green trough that cradles Budd Lake. Before it became the winding strip of camping, snowmobiling and just kickin' back resorts that it is now, it took its turn as a center of commerce and debauchery during the virtual Brazilian waxing of the state's majestic white pines. While wealthy lumber speculators were reaping the sawdust rush from their lush, taxidermied dens in Denver, Saginaw or Boston, a steady flow of able-bodied men arrived. Lumbering was something that promised a roof, a bed, three squares through the coldest months of the year and a paycheck just when the weather was turning gentler. The workers came from out East, drawn by newspaper want ads, straight from Ellis Island, or fresh from parole.

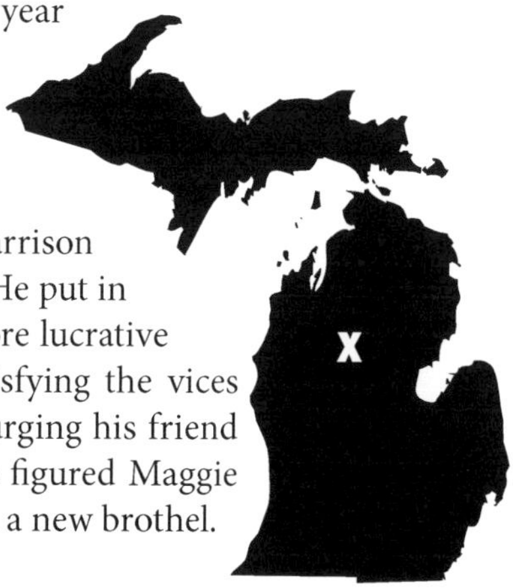

James Carr was in his mid-20s when he came to Harrison from Rochester, New York, to work in a lumber camp. He put in his time, but eventually figured out that it would be more lucrative and less physically demanding to make his living satisfying the vices of the wood cutters. He sent word back to Rochester, urging his friend Maggie Duncan to join him in the wild northwest. He figured Maggie could be the boss or madam and his business partner in a new brothel.

Now, there were women who gravitated to that line of work on their own and saw opportunity in catering to the drunken, female-companionship-starved lumber workers. There were also those that were bamboozled with ads in Detroit and Toledo, ads that claimed to be seeking hotel maids or cooks. Worse yet, some were drugged and kidnapped in places like rough-and-tumble Saginaw, then brought to the muddy mayhem of the northern lumber towns to be sex slaves. There were likely many more ways of coercing or tricking women into a life of prostitution, and some of the practitioners even ended up in court for it. Maggie Duncan, for instance, at one time faced criminal charges because she "compelled Jennie Handley to be defiled," according to one of the criminal cases against her.

Even those who opposed the sin industry — the farmers, merchants and others there to make an honest living, and their pastors — generally offered the women little help or sympathy. They snickered behind their backs and looked down their noses at them on the street. It was a miserable life as one of society's cast-offs. Some of the more desperate women felt that their only chance to escape was to guzzle down some over-the-counter opiates and end it all — an all-too-common occurrence in their line of work.

Local doctors would periodically bring their satchels to the whorehouses, and check the women for sexually transmitted diseases. The proprietors were in favor of the checkups, since an outbreak would be bad for business. So if someone was found to be infected, she might have to be sent packing.

For the most part, the only real effort by the law to deal with the problem was to fine the powerless women for plying their trade. The fines were set out of their reach and so they'd end up being shipped by wagon or train to the Midland jail for a spell. That was the nearest jail, since Clare County was wrangling over the price of building its own hoose gow, something the Jim Carrs and Maggie Duncans of the community were perfectly happy not having around.

So when the tired, hungry, spring-bitten jacks finally got a wad of cash after the final thaw, the young couple from the Empire State was ready to help them spend it. Carr and Duncan ran the happiest place on earth for the newly free and paid. Liquor and women at the "Devil's Ranch" was the promise. Every so often, there was a guy who didn't make it to that promised land because he'd guzzled or gagged down too much of the hard stuff. He passed out, allowing Carr, Duncan or one of their goons to rummage through his pockets, then toss him out in the mud. Losing his annual salary meant the poor sap had just endured a winter of frozen sweat and an icicled beard for beans, a bed and one bad drinking spree.

Carr and Duncan took their ill-gotten gains and paid it forward, right into the hand of Clare County Sheriff John S. Cramer. So it's not too surprising that if a lumberman stumbled over to the law to report his shabby treatment, the officials would be about as sympathetic as an axe handle.

The Carr-Duncan empire thrived in spite of the pair's reputation for treacherous customer relations, and survived extensive competition. There's said to have been more than 20 houses of ill repute in the county run by both women and men in those days. While the commerce of the frolic went on behind closed doors, there was liquor in the front. Now, several other counties in the region had voted to go dry, but a traveling man could always stop in the lumber towns and slam back a few gut warmers. Satisfying those baser appetites has always been a winning business model, and the Devil's Ranch was the biggest taxpayer in Clare County at its apex.

Carr's alleged antics became a campaign issue in 1884. While the country was electing President Grover Cleveland for the first time, the county was figuring they'd give George Graham a chance at wearing the sheriff's star. He and prosecutor candidate William A. Burritt ran victoriously as Democrats on a law-and-order platform. The names of Maggie Duncan and James Carr came up in more than a few of their campaign discussions on the topic of immorality, while talking to the staid and proper settlers.

And so, the tough young couple, whom people whispered about behind their backs with gossip of robbery and murder, became frequent subjects of the court docket. The women in the employ of their house and similar establishments, scorned by the "decent" folk, were also frequent guests on the wrong side of the bench. Usually as defendants, but sometimes as victims.

Remember that Hinkley's Bone Liniment

Is no "fad" in medicine, but that for fifty years it has been continuously proving that it is a certain and quick specific, when taken internally, for Colds, Coughs, Croup, Sore Throat, Diphtheria, Tonsilitis, Asthma, Catarrh, Bronchitis, Inflammation of the Lungs, Acid Stomach, Dyspepsia, Indigestion, Heartburn, Cramps, Colic, Painter's Colic, Worms, Cholera, Diarrhœa, Sick Headache, Fever and Ague, Liver and Kidney Troubles, Canker Mouth and Nervous Debility.

Applied externally for Acute, Sciatic, Muscular and Chronic Rheumatism, Rheumatic Gout, Neuralgia, Headache, Toothache, Pain in the Back or Loins, Lumbago, Erysipelas, Chilblains, Frostbites, Old Sores, Ringworms, Whitlows, Sprains, Bruises, Wounds, Burns, Stings of Insects and Bites of Venomous Reptiles.

Only 25 cents a bottle, and every bottle a veritable "family medicine chest" in itself. Full directions, which are exceedingly simple, on every bottle.

Don't cost much to try, so wouldn't it be foolish for us to make claims we could not fulfil? Only try it and you'll find Hinkley's Bone Liniment is better than we claim. The druggist has it or will quickly get it for you.

Remember that for every pain to which mankind is liable there is positive and almost instant relief found in Hinkley's Bone Liniment—and only 25 cents a bottle.

[illegible] Bone Liniment Co., Saginaw, Mich., U. [illegible]

As the jacks spent the winter work season dreaming of spring, they had year-round vices to get them through the back pain of lumbering and the irritation of bunkmates. Many took solace in Hinkley's Bone Liniment out of Saginaw. It and other high-alcohol cures and over-the-counter opiates were readily available to treat rheumatoid arthritis and general body aches. Or maybe just to feed an increasing craving for high-alcohol cures and over-the-counter opiates. Jacks, women of the evening and disillusioned pioneers could stroll into a general store or apothecary to self-medicate. They regularly tossed the bottles in the woods and former woods, so a lot of old medicine bottles have turned up around former lumber-boom sites.

In this transient society, bartenders were at least as tough as the customers. Fires were frequent, as was arson. One was set in Harrison in 1886 by someone who had been refused a room in an inn. It destroyed an entire block, including a restaurant, a barber shop and a general store.

The above photo shows the wreckage of the J. W. Wells Lumber Company of Menominee. It burned to the ground on April 13, 1931, and was one of the biggest fires in the U.S. that year.

WE DON'T KNOW WHERE YOUNG FRANKIE OSBORN HAD COME FROM BEFORE SHE HAD THE MISFORTUNE OF WORKING FOR THE GREEDY COUPLE AS A PROSTITUTE. She apparently had that one trait that a pimp can't abide in "his women": a strong will. One evening, as the house began to fill with fragrant loggers, Frankie sat in a corner, feeling nauseous and out of sorts. She caught the eye of one of the hard-ridden, wool-clad laborers nonetheless. There were other hostesses milling about, but as the fiddler sawed away at his tunes, the customer lost sight of the rest of the crowd and walked over to Frankie. Hat in hand, he politely asked her to dance. "Thanks, but I don't feel well," she told him. He stepped back with a hangdog nod.

Unfortunately for Frankie, though, the manager was watching. Carr came over to ask why she was snubbing the clientele. Words turned to fists, shoves and smacks. Men and women stood stunned and uncomfortable. Carr motioned one of his bouncers over. "Finish her," he said.

Maybe out of mercy — or he just wasn't taking the boss literally — the thug did not "finish her." Nonetheless, the "girls" knew it was a message to all of them. *This joint can't afford to give sick time off, and don't cross the boss.* The men knew it was none of their affair and some of them may have felt so awkward about it that they hastened their trip to an upstairs boudoir with one of Frankie's co-workers, just to get away from the unpleasantness.

For the next few nights, Carr stewed over the mouthy little whore who dared talk back to him. We'll never know what ignited the inevitable last spark, but a few nights later Carr saw another opening to let her have it. One of the other women took her to her room to protect and mother her. She died the next day.

Carr was not popular with others in his line of work, either.

Peter McCarthy had a competing saloon, and when he bought 40 acres next to the town of Meredith, Carr saw the potential of big-time competition. Carr warned him that if he opened a brothel there, unpleasant things might happen. McCarthy wasn't going to be intimidated. Walls started going up and new women rode the train in from Saginaw. Carr seethed, but as far as anyone knows for sure, he never approached his new competitor again. Not much later, however, saloon-owner William Villaneuve shot the newcomer over a 10-cent bar tab. McCarthy had said the beer he'd just drunk wasn't worth a dime, so Villaneuve pulled his piece from behind the bar and shot him dead. Many wondered whether the pistol-packing bartender was in cahoots with Carr.

Not that it ended up mattering too much. Carr was getting in deeper and deeper for other things, as well. For one, another competitor's house burned down under the cloying aroma of kerosene and with Jim Carr's foot soldiers having been seen nearby.

THE MOST EXPLOSIVE ALLEGATIONS ABOUT CARR WERE SPILLED BY A SHORT-TERM, MIDLAND CELLMATE OF HIS.

Harry Jones lay sleepless near the stove at Carr's house. Who knows why he chose to unload his conscience on James Lapham. The two were sharing a bed near the stove, because traveling strangers had to do that sometimes. Lapham was up from Lowell — upriver of Grand Rapids on the Grand — for a meeting. Whether Jones blurted out his guilt right away, or whether he led up to it in conversation, with the help of gulps off a bottle, he shifted the conversation to the weight on his shoulders.

"If that stove could talk, it would tell a sad tale," he said.

He went on to narrate how he'd met the infamous James Carr in Midland County Jail, among Clare County's other miscreants and whores. The political winds were shifting in Clare and Harrison, and Carr was seeing more of the inside of a cell and courtroom. In Jones, Carr must have recognized a sympathetic ear, or a sucker who could be manipulated. They sat in the cell and had a long talk, aided with "all the whiskey they could drink," Jones later said.

Carr waxed on about his exploits and business acumen, and eventually got around to telling him of a body in a barrel in a shallow, sandy grave, not too far from a house that liked to keep its curtains closed. The body was someone who'd gotten on his bad side. It was also damning evidence, and Carr needed to have it destroyed. When Jones asked the name of the unfortunate person whose body he'd be burning down to a few bone shards, Carr laughed and looked away. "There's nothing in a name," he said.

The crooked saloonkeeper also asked that he shoot sheriff's Deputy Andrew Mack in the back. For Jones's troubles, on both matters, he would earn $500. Jones considered either of those chores alone to be above and beyond the call of nasty, but 500 bucks could get him a long ways further west.

As Carr, the keeper of kidnapped women, pleaded with Jones to do the dirty deeds, he tearily took Jones's hand and said, "My life and liberty lies in your hands." When Jones finally agreed, Carr urged him, "For God's sake, don't write to me or mention my name."

Jones was halfway done with those chores when he met Lapham. He'd chosen the grisly burning of bones and rancid muscle as the first of his tasks. Yet as that escapade gnawed at his conscience, he seriously didn't want to take out an officer of the law. If he didn't, though, he didn't know what Carr, or someone indebted to Carr, might do to him.

However that would turn out, Jones needed to unload the burden that was souring his stomach. So Jones grabbed a lantern and led Lapham out for a dark tour. The snow was "pretty much thawed off" around the house, but there was still eight or 10 inches in the woods. They came to the sandy clearing where Jones told him he had dug up the grave and removed the barrel. "There are six more under here," he said. Lapham listened, staying alert and keeping his eyes on this man sharing the secrets he hadn't asked to hear.

Jones then took him to a barn and showed him some steel hoops. They were, he explained, all that was left of the barrel that had acted as a crude casket.

He told him how he removed the cover of the barrel and puked from the stench of the maggot-infested corpse. He chopped up the unknown man's bones, so they'd fit in the stove, and burned the body and the putrefied barrel staves, piece by piece. It took him the entire night.

And now, he'd wished he hadn't done it. What's more, he didn't plan to pull off the last part of the deal. Burning someone who was already dead was one thing, but killing someone, a lawman, was quite another.

Whether Jones hoped the stranger would keep his secret or tell the authorities to bring an honest end to it is hard to say. Lapham did the latter. Before he headed back to Lowell, Lapham found a lawman and told him of the "sad tale" Jones had burdened him with.

JONES GOT A CHANCE TO TELL THE STORY AGAIN IN COURT, AS HE AND CARR FACED CHARGES. Townspeople wanted to see Carr brought down, and not just for his obvious sins. The settlers were often at odds with the drinking and carousing of the lumberjacks and the businesses built around depravity and debauchery that they attracted. Church sermons railed against the drinking and whoring, but the tree-cutters were determined to spend their money and free time the way they wanted.

It wasn't just the caliber of recreation that irritated the settlers. The lumber company owners were also cheating the townspeople on taxes. Farmland was assessed at as high as 90 percent of its worth, while timberland was assessed as low as 3 percent. A white pine growers association flexed its muscle to keep it that way.

In fact, the tax dispute helped put off building a county jail for about six years in the mid-1880s. That was the six-year window in which Carr took free reign to terrorize anyone who crossed him, surround himself with ruffians who would just as soon slice your jugular as look at you, and pay off greedy and spineless politicians to keep the gravy train rolling.

And so, in 1883 or '84, the new settlement of Meredith was platted out by Thomas McClennon in the northeastern part of the county, further than Harrison from the law and the growing outcry over the entertainment offered to thirsty, horny and sometimes violent lumbermen. McClennon set himself up to control the flow of liquor in town, and keep his own palms well-greased.

Carr and Duncan knew a good opportunity when they saw one. They opened a new franchise there.

Yet at the same time, Carr's name appeared more and more in county court documents. A guy named Gaffney, who repeatedly threw rocks at another man until he knocked him unconscious, was identified as an employee of Carr's. In another case, a fiddler employed by Carr was charged with stealing a patron's wallet. One document speculates that the association may have inspired a juror not to show up for fear of retaliation. A woman suing her husband for divorce cited a witness who saw him joking around with the ladies at Carr and Duncan's on his lap, and then going upstairs with one of them for a half hour. Carr himself was charged with beating a woman on the head with a club.

But the heat was rising mostly for the body that Harry Jones burned. A sliver or two of unburned bone was all the *corpus* they could *habeas*, but they also had the word of Jones. They decided the victim was a guy by the name of Charles Corbin, whoever he was. The motive and the victim's identity remain uncertain.

Still, with the new sheriff and changing political climate, the murder charge finally came. They figured they should probably take down Maggie with him, so they charged her with operating a bawdy house.

THEY WERE CONVICTED, THOUGH THEY EACH ONLY SERVED A YEAR IN PRISON. THEN THEY BOTH RETURNED TO TOWN TO RESUME THEIR OLD LIVES.

It's been said that they even tried to open a new business like the old one. How they thought they'd succeed is a mystery. There may have been remnants of the region's lumber days, but for the most part, the barons and the couple's main clientele had moved further north, where the white pines were still plentiful.

Yet the two remained in Meredith, likely wracked by addictions and disillusionment, waiting for their inglorious final breaths. It came for both of them in 1892, within hours of each other, in a freezing shack near Meredith, as March in Michigan did its cruel tease, wavering between mud and back to frozen mud.

The local newspaper practically gloated about them lying in the wooden shack, trying to ride out March next to a stove with no wood. An unnamed companion sat with the couple, supposedly to watch over them in their illness and frailty. As they drifted in and out of their last fever dreams, the stranger glugged down their only remaining source of comfort, a bottle of rot-gut whiskey. About the time that James settled into the death rattle, the vagrant visitor tipped up the last warming drop and left for town, and a doctor. The physician declared James dead. Maggie followed suit within hours.

The *Clare Democrat and Press* eulogized the pair on page one, Friday, March 25, 1892: "Though the lives of both were plentifully interspersed with acts of open handed charity in the days of their prosperity, still the evil so predominated in their general make-up that all that was good was sunk from sight and will only be called to mind by the great Bookkeeper in making out His balance sheet with these two miserably spent lives."

It ended with a verse as cold as their frozen corpses:

Rattle his bones
Over the stones,
For he's only a pauper,
Whom nobody owns.

HELICOPTER HIJACK

THE YEAR: 1975
THE CRIME: PRISON ESCAPE
THE MOTIVE: PRISON SUCKS

PRISONERS AND GUARDS WERE STUNNED ON A JUNE DAY WHEN A HELICOPTER APPROACHED THE EXERCISE YARD AT A SOUTHERN MICHIGAN PRISON. IT FLUTTERED OVER THE RAZOR WIRE AND GUN TOWER. ITS PROPELLERS BLEW THE GRASS AND DUST IN A SWIRL AS IT TOUCHED DOWN, RIGHT THERE, SMACK DAB IN THE MIDDLE OF THE SUNSHINE AND FRESH AIR/PSYCHOLOGICAL WAR ZONE THAT IS THE YARD OF A STATE PRISON.

Everyone was surprised. Everyone, that is, except Dale Otto Remling.

Remling, serving time for forgery and trying to sell stolen hogs, jogged over to the cockpit and hopped in. Slack-jawed inmates and guards watched as the whirly-bird carried Remling to freedom.

Remling had had a long career of writing bad checks and money-making con games. And he'd already escaped the prison bars of California, twice; he fled to Michigan's Montcalm County to resume his shady ways in the Midwest. From there, he went down to Hooper, Nebraska, and locked 11 people in a truck trailer, then took off in a rig carrying 383 hogs worth more than $70,000 in bacon, chops and hams. He managed to drive the living, smelling cargo to Iowa. He couldn't sell them at market there, though. He didn't have the required paperwork.

So back to Michigan he came and continued to pass bad checks until he was caught forging a $2,400 check to buy a car. He was locked in Jackson for fraud. About that same time, Nebraska convicted him for the pork caper. He was warehoused here but was marking long days for both states. Still, he apparently had pretty good contact with the outside, as he enlisted several free criminals to plan the escape that was to set him apart. It was proceeding flawlessly, but the helicopter ride was just the first leg of what was to have been a truly epic conspiracy. It was to involve several ride changes to throw police off the scent on the way to a Lansing hotel room meeting.

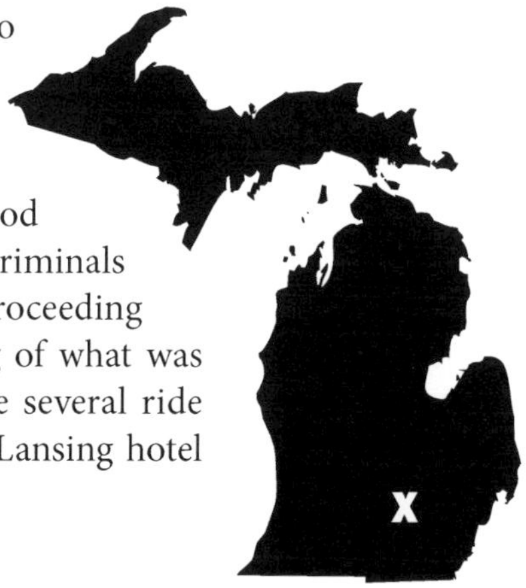

X

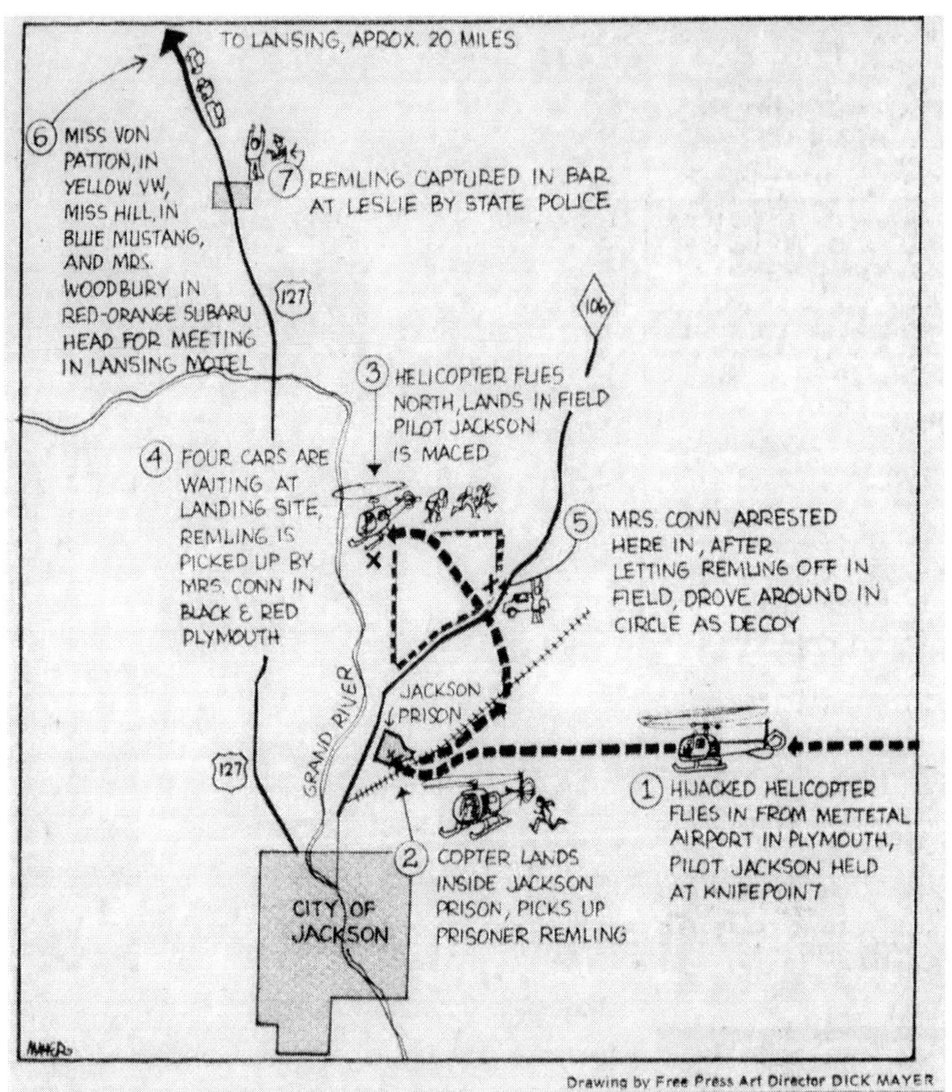

Detroit Free Press: Jun 8, 1975.

Some wondered if it was a copycat crime, taken from a recent Charles Bronson action flick called “Breakout.” And here’s the best part: the prison had just looped the movie through a projector to show it to inmates a few days before Remling’s cinematic moment. I know, right?

Despite the grand exit, however, what happened after the chopper flew out of sight was anything but grand.

As the copter, owned by a charter service in Plymouth, made its landing for the first leg of the land voyage, either Remling or the hijacker sprayed the acidic sting of mace into the 29-year-old pilot’s eyes.

But the plan may have contained too many moving parts. Remling missed or ditched one of his rides and was left to wander confused for

The 1975 movie "Breakout" was shown in a Jackson theater just a week prior to the real deal.

a day or so. Then, police followed an anonymous tip to Huffie's Bar in Leslie, a mere 15 miles from the prison. They converged on the tavern.

A grin spread across Remling's face as he saw the police. He set down bags of groceries he was carrying and presented his wrists to his captors.

Some of the press and public expressed admiration for the chutzpah of the stunt. And Remling told reporters he kept escaping because he hated prisons: "I think cages are for something other than people. You talk about problems with people, the prison system breeds it into you."

But then again, nobody told him to write those bad checks.

ACKNOWLEDGMENTS

It would be impossible to write a book like this, or any book for that matter, in a vacuum. There's no way to fully convey my appreciation and dependence upon the help of others, whether it's people who have knowingly and specifically helped me, or have written about or kept official records of these stories in the past.

I don't know if it's possible to thank everyone who has helped in this effort, and I apologize if I've missed anyone. So here is my attempt to recognize all of my partners in true crime, so to speak.

Thanks to Phil Schertzing for his historical knowledge of the Michigan State Police and bringing certain stories to my attention.

While the electronic word may be changed by people with ill intent, libraries are invaluable resources to all of us, as repositories of our shared knowledge and a preserver of the hard copies of the written word that will hopefully continue to survive intact for centuries to come. The one closest to me, geographically, the one I've used most often, is Traverse Area District Library. A special shoutout to Robin Stanley, who has readily helped me most often on my many questions, though all of the staff there has been eager and able to assist whenever needed. Also, I extend gratitude to the Library of Michigan in Lansing, with its tremendous collection of newspapers on microfilm, saving them from the brittle fate of paper itself, and for its extensive records of statewide and local significance.

Historical societies in local communities also help to bring the past to life. Ronald Barwick and Beverly Johnson of the Bellaire Museum have been of particular importance in helping piece together chronology and geography in the Mancelona robbery. In the cases of the Smalley brothers and James Carr/Maggie Duncan, Jon Rigelberg of the Clare County Historical Society has helped me, and others in the future, by preserving, organizing and electronically transcribing old court records for posterity. Thanks also to Meredith Slover, Curator of Collections at Tri-Cities Historical Museum in Grand Haven, as well as the staff of the Royal Oak Historical Society. In Clarkston, thank you to Toni Smith of Clarkston

Community Historical Society & Heritage Museum for access to that organization's records, as well as Sarah Schneider, owner of The Fed, a restaurant in what once was the local bank, for giving me a tour that helped to visualize the robbery there.

Many thanks to Jim Donahue of the Mitten Word bookshop in Marshall, and Fred H. Cummins formerly of the Battle Creek police, for background and story ideas.

Also, thanks to David Ashenfelter of the Eastern Michigan District of the U.S. District Court, the Bloomfield Township Police Department and the Wisconsin Division of Criminal Investigation of the Wisconsin State Police.

Of course, I must give my everlasting gratitude to my wife Maria for her patience and support through the long process of writing a book, as well as for listening to me read stories and helping to fine tune the language. In addition, friends have lent an ear to some of the pieces, and have given their opinions and direction, including Heather Palmer and Ron and Carol Carr (there's that name again), who are also not related to me, and I say that for their benefit, not mine.

And I must also thank the best little publishing company in the world, Mission Point Press. Heather Shaw, thank you for your editing and design on this book. Anne Gertiser Stanton, thank you for the critical eye and for all you and your husband Doug Stanton do for authors in Traverse City and elsewhere. And Doug Weaver, thank you for technical and business direction and for all you've taught me about the business of books. And thanks to all of you for your guidance and support of and faith in me and this project.

TO READ MORE, LOOK FOR THESE TITLES

Assassination of a Michigan King: the Life of James Jesse Strang, by Roger Van Noord

Autobiography of a Stagecoach Robber: The Saga of Reimund Holzhey, by Bruce K. Cox

Baby Face Nelson: Portrait of a Public Enemy, by Steven Nickel and William J. Helmer

Boudoirs to Brothels: The Intimate World of Wild West Women, by Michael Rutter

Company Towns of Michigan's Upper Peninsula, by Christian Holmes

The Detroit True Crime Chronicles: Tales of Murder and Mayhem in the Motor City, by Scott M. Burnstein

The Dillinger Days, by John Toland

A Duty to Honor, A Duty to Remember: A Tribute to Michigan Sheriffs & Deputy Sheriffs Who Have Made the Ultimate Sacrifice, by Timothy Coe

The Historical Atlas of American Crime, by Fred Rosen

A History of Heists: Bank Robbery in America, by Jerry Clark and Ed Palattella

Justus S. Stearns: Michigan Pine King and Kentucky Coal Baron, 1845-1933, by Michael W. Nagle

The King of Beaver Island, by C.K. Backus

The King Strang Story: A vindication of James J. Strang, the Beaver Island Mormon King, by Doyle C. Fitzpatrick

Lost Towns of Eastern Michigan, by Alan Naldrett

Michigan's Lumbertowns: Lumbermen and Laborers in Saginaw, Bay City and Muskegon, 1870-1905, by Jeremy W. Kilar

Michigan's Timber Battleground, A History of Clare County: 1674-1900, by Forrest B. Meek

Murder & Mayhem in Grand Rapids, by Tobin T. Buhk

The New York Times Book of Crime: More than 166 Years of Covering the Beat, edited by Kevin Flynn

Outlaws of the Lakes: Bootlegging & Smuggling from Colonial Times to Prohibition, by Edward Butts

Police Technology: 21st-Century Crime-Fighting Tools (Law Enforcement and Intelligence Gathering), by Glen C Forrest

Public Enemies: America's Greatest Crime Wave and the Birth of the FBI, 1933-34, by Bryan Burrough

Soiled Doves: Prostitution in the Early West (Women of the West), by Anne Seagraves

Stick 'Em Up: Michigan Bank Robberies of the 1920s & 1930s, by Tom Powers

Still on the Beat: A History of the Battle Creek Police Department, by Fred H. Cummins

True Crime: Michigan: The State's Most Notorious Criminal Cases, by Tobin T. Buhk

Upstairs Girls: Prostitution in the American West, by Michael Rutter

Illustration of an early Erie & Kalamazoo train.

ABOUT THE AUTHOR

TOM CARR is an independent writer and journalist in Northern Michigan who spent 25 years in daily newspapers, primarily the *Traverse City Record-Eagle*. He's won journalistic awards for his investigative reporting, feature writing, breaking news and humor columns. Carr often covered police, courts and crime and reported closely on some memorable and well-known crimes.

As a freelancer, Carr has branched out into other media and has reported and produced many stories for Interlochen Public Radio and has had his work broadcast on NPR and Michigan Radio, as well. His work has appeared in the *Detroit Free Press*, the *New York Daily News*, traverseticker.com, *Traverse Magazine*, and other media.

Tom Carr is author of *Blood on the Mitten: Infamous Michigan Murders, 1700s-Present* and was a contributing writer for *Inside Upnorth: The Complete Tour, Sport and Country Living Guide to Traverse City, Traverse City Area, Leelanau County*, also published by Mission Point Press.

Carr lives near Buckley, Michigan with his wife, Maria, where they raised their two sons.

INDEX

BOY'S WOUND MAY BE A FATAL ONE

FRANK TEBEAU.

Port Huron, Mich., October 23.—Hovering between life and death, with his body peppered with shot, Frank Tebeau, of Marine City, lies on a cot at the City hospital. The boy was shot while in the alleged act of stealing grapes from an arbor at the home of Captain William H. Brown at Marine City and his condition was today reported as critical. It is said that the attending physicians are unable to locate the small shot which entered the boy's body. The sheriff is waiting for a change in the boy's condition before a warrant is sworn out for Brown.

Detroit Free Press; Oct 24, 1907.

Tragic End to a Love Story.

CINCINNATI, O., Dec. 30.—[Special.]—Eighteen-year-old Fannie Buchert was sent by her wealthy parents in Austria three months ago to her uncle, Julius Waldner, in this city in order to break off a love match. She has been writing to her lover and a recent letter from him said he had been unable to save money to come to America. Last night the girl arrayed herself in bridal robes and took arsenic. She was found dead this morning.

Murder in Michigan.

Michigan's murder roll for 1892 is the largest in the State's history.

Hair Stockings.

Stockings made of human hair are worn by Chinese fishermen as a preventive against wet feet.

£1,000,000.

The Bank of England once issued two notes of a million pounds each. Two rich Englishmen—brothers—fell into a dispute as to what would become of an honest stranger turned adrift in London with no money but one of these million-pound bank-notes, and no way to account for his being in possession of it.

MARK TWAIN.

"Brother A said he would starve to death; Brother B said he would n't. Brother A said he could n't offer it at a bank or anywhere else, because he would be arrested on the spot. So they went on disputing till Brother B said he would bet twenty thousand pounds that the man would live thirty days, *any way*, on that million, and keep out of jail, too. Brother A took him up. Brother B went down to the bank and bought the note. Then they sat at the window a whole day watching for the right man to give it to."

How they found the man—a young American—and his adventures with the note, are fully related in the story

"The £1,000,000 Bank-Note,"

BY

MARK TWAIN.

One of the great humorist's best inventions,—complete in the

JAN'Y CENTURY

THIS YOUNG MAN ACTS NERVOUSLY.

He Walks Many Blocks Before Examining His Prize, Which He Keeps.

It is an easy thing to lose a pocketbook. Even a man can do it as readily, if not as artistically, as a woman when he makes up his mind to the rashness. But the loss wears more on the constitution of a man, partly because the sensation is a novel one, and therefore he broods over it; partly because it is a reflection on his business capacity, but mostly because he soon concludes that any one who will carry a pocketbook for

HE EXAMINES HIS FIND.

dimes and nickels and pennies is an idiot at the best. Such a gathering of small change is an invitation to ill-luck and the expert pickpocket.

MORE FROM MISSION POINT PRESS

CURRENT AFFAIRS

POISON ON TAP:
How Government Failed Flint and the Heroes Who Fought Back
A Bridge Magazine Analysis of the Flint water crisis.
Sometimes truth is stranger and scarier than fiction—such is the case with the Flint Water Crisis. Bridge Magazine staff painstakingly document one of the most significant cases of environmental injustice in U.S. history. —Marc Edwards, Virginia Tech professor whose work helped prove that the regulators were wrong

THE INTERSECTION:
What Detroit has gained, and lost, 50 years after the uprisings of 1967
By Bridge Magazine
and The Detroit Journalism Collective
Fifty years after anger and frustration over police-community relations boiled over into a rebellion in Detroit, there are lots of people asking what we've learned, how we've changed. This book, a collection of the coverage by the Detroit Journalism Cooperative during 2016, is a testament to that. — From the Foreword by Pulitzer Prize-winning, Detroit native Stephen Henderson

PEACE IN JUSTICE:
Reflections from a Career in the Criminal Justice System
By Carol Getty
One part memoir and one part essay, *Peace in Justice* offers an insightful analysis of the American criminal justice system by someone who spent decades working in the state and federal systems. Carol Getty's illustrative career took her from the Arizona Board of Pardons and Paroles to the highest office of the United States Parole Commission.

AND CHANDLER LAKE BOOKS

HISTORY

BLOOD ON THE MITTEN:
Infamous Michigan Murders, 1700s to Present
By Tom Carr
In this hugely effective debut, Tom Carr sheds keen illumination upon a regional inventory of killers, kooks, cutthroats and the aggressively unhinged. The tales are horrific and humorous by turns — grisly, goofy, poignant dispatches expertly summated by a skilled veteran reporter who's no stranger to the back stairs habituated by a true sleuth. Story telling at its fully imagined best."
— Ben Hamper, bestselling author of *Rivethead*

HOW THE GOOD TIMES ROLLED:
What We Did Before the Digital Age
By Richard Fidler
Believe it or not, a hundred years ago, people connected directly, face-to-face, for fun and friendship. Dozens of archival photos from the Grand Traverse Area.

INSIDE UPNORTH:
The Complete Tour, Sport and Country Living Guide to Traverse City, Traverse City Area and Leelanau County
By Heather Shaw, Jodee Taylor, Tom Carr and many others
Whether you're planning a visit, are new to the area or you've lived here your whole life, INSIDE UPNORTH is an indispensable go-to road map to all things wonderful in Northwest Michigan.

MORE FROM MISSION POINT PRESS

NATURE

OF THINGS IGNORED AND UNLOVED:
A Naturalist Walks Northern Michigan
By Richard Fidler
This book will awaken the reader to events and things tuned out and forgotten in the noisy, rushing environment of our lives. It is a safari to nearby places.
"There are no insignificant beings, as Fidler so beautifully shows us.: —Fleda Brown, poet and essayist

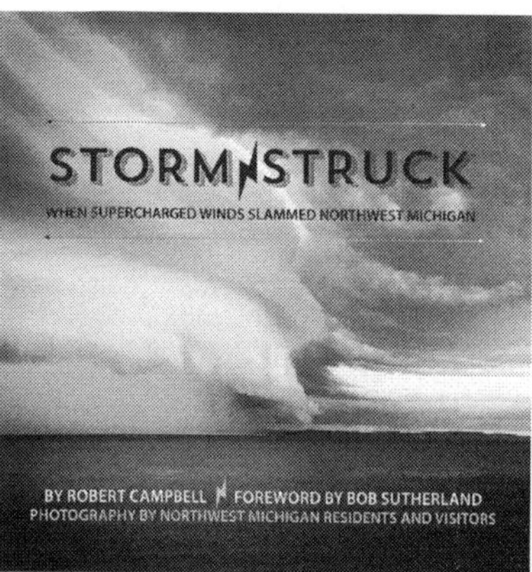

STORM STRUCK:
When Supercharged Winds Slammed Northwest Michigan
By Robert Campbell; Foreword by Bob Sutherland
Photography by northwest Michigan residents and visitors

LEELANAU BY KAYAK:
Day Trips, Pics, Tips and Stories of a Beautiful Michigan Peninsula
By Jon R. Constant
with Larry Burns
Beautiful photographs illustrate the lakeshore, Leelanau's many interior lakes and its three rivers. Up to date directions and tips for all ages and expertise. Includes some maps.

AND CHANDLER LAKE BOOKS

BIOGRAPHY & MEMOIR

HOBEY BAKER: UPON FURTHER REVIEW
Exploring the Life and Death of a Hockey Immortal
By Tim Rappleye

He was America's most dashing athlete, the pride of Princeton. Hobey Baker, the aristocratic Ivy League sports hero and, later, a glamorous World War I fighter pilot. From the outside, U.S. Army Captain Hobey Baker had it all: good looks, a glamorous fiancé, war medals for bravery, and a sports resume second to none. And then it all came crashing down, barely a month following the Armistice.

HOW THIN THE VEIL:
A Memoir of 45 Days in the Traverse City State Hospital
By Jack Kerkhoff
with an introduction by Ray Minervini
How Thin the Veil is a 45-day account of Kerkhoff's treatment, his conversations with the nurses and doctors (some of them with their real names), his interactions with the inmates, and his trips to downtown Traverse City watering holes. There's also romance in the form of Suzy, a pretty, lisping waif whose "bad spells" had kept her hospitalized for eight years. First published in 1952, How Thin the Veil shines a "hard-boiled" light on the mid-century conditions of patients of mental illness.

THE GOOD HIKE:
A Story of the Appalachian Trail, PTSD, and Love
By Tim Keenan
The Good Hike is the story of a journey from Georgia to Maine in the shadow of the Vietnam war. It's a story of resilience, of goodness, of camaraderie, love, and of a man trying to find peace within his post traumatic stress disorder (PTSD).

MORE FROM MISSION POINT PRESS

HOW TO

GOING OUT GREEN:
One Man's Adventure Planning His Own Natural Burial
by Bob Butz
Bob Butz, investigative reporter, humorist, and amateur naturalist is on assignment: He's planning his own natural burial in three months.
"At once elegant and funny as hell, Bob Butz has written the most useful book I've seen all year. Everyone will be needing this book. No exceptions. See you at sunset." — Doug Peacock, author of *Grizzly Years: In Search of the American Wilderness*

HUSTLE 'TIL IT HAPPENS:
Turning Bold Dreams Into Reality
By Sam Flamont
"Hustle 'Til It Happens provides great guidance, and the right amount of motivation, to help anyone define their goals, develop the disciplines to achieve them, and recognize that they have the power within themselves to make their dreams a reality. If you're feeling stuck, or not living the life you wanted to live, pick up this book and start taking action today." — Angie Morgan, *New York Times* Best Selling author of *Spark: How to Lead Yourself and Others to Greater Success and Leading from the Front*

ON A PIT AND A PRAYER:
How I Grew a Business, Lost a Business, and Found Faith, Family and Love
By Michelle White
"This is a great read for any small business owner or aspiring small business owner. Many perils await in the mine field that is small business ownership, and Michelle survived them all. She takes us on a journey of passion, heart, loss and love. We have much to learn from her experiences!" — Cammie Buehler, Managing Partner, Epicure Catering & Cherry Basket Farm

AND CHANDLER LAKE BOOKS

MYSTERY & THRILLER

THE CENTER CANNOT HOLD

By Aaron Stander

In the depths of winter, Cedar County is on occasion literally frozen in place. Roads are impassable; the area schools are closed for days at a time. And the bad guys and gals, they're hunkered down like everyone else until the weather breaks. But this winter isn't the usual. There's arson and murder. The iniquities of some particularly unsavory ancestors are being visited upon the current generation.

DEATH LEASE

By Peter Marabell

In 1922, Augustus Sanderson hired Charles W. Caskey, architect of Grand Hotel, to build a "majestic cottage" high on the East Bluff of Mackinac Island. Camille Sanderson, like her ancestors, assumed responsibility for the cottage when her turn came. Camille turns to private investigator Michael Russo when her ex-husband steals the lease. So begins a journey awash in deception, forgery, murder and lies.

OPERATION LIGHT SWITCH

By John Wemlinger

"John Wemlinger has written a fast-moving and compelling story of overcoming a grave injustice with the help of family, friends, caring military professionals, and sheer guts."
— Ron Christmas, Lieutenant General, USMC (Ret)

"Wemlinger gets it. The nimbleness of our armed forces is as important today as its fire power. *Operation Light Switch* is a great read. Enjoyed it from cover to cover." — Mike Kelleher, Brigadier General, US Army (Ret)

Made in the USA
Coppell, TX
13 October 2022

84585122R00076